ARCHITECTURAL DETAILS

ARCHITECTURAL
DETAILS

ARCHITECTURAL DETAILS

MARCIA REISS

THUNDER BAY
P · R · E · S · S

San Diego, California

Thunder Bay Press
An imprint of the Advantage Publishers Group
5880 Oberlin Drive, San Diego, CA 92121-4794
www.thunderbaybooks.com

Produced by PRC Publishing Limited,
The Chrysalis Building
Bramley Road, London W10 6SP, United Kingdom

An imprint of **Chrysalis** Books Group

All notations of errors or omissions should be addressed to Thunder Bay Press,
Editorial Department, at the above address. All other correspondence (author inquiries,
permissions) concerning the content of this book should be addressed to
PRC Publishing Limited, The Chrysalis Building, Bramley Road, London W10 6SP,
United Kingdom.

ISBN 1-59223-201-9

Library of Congress Cataloging-in-Publication Data available upon request.

Printed and bound in Malaysia

1 2 3 4 5 08 07 06 05 04

CONTENTS

CHAPTER I
AMERICAN ARCHITECTURAL STYLES

God is in the details.

—Ludwig Mies van der Rohe

American architecture has no single style, nor has it ever had one. It is as complex and rich as the history of the nation and its people. Native Americans and immigrants from all parts of the world have imprinted their culture in buildings of amazing diversity. They have created infinite variations in every building component, from basic windows, doors, and roofs, to elaborate ornamentation. The history of American architecture unfolds in these details. Each one tells its own story of social and cultural change, industrial development, and the esthetic and ideological choices Americans have made in the places they live, worship, and work.

Waves of eclectic styles have washed over American architecture. The nation's homes, houses of worship, and civic buildings bear the features of Greek and Roman temples, medieval churches and castles, Italian villas, and French châteaux—even Egyptian pyramids. In the heyday of eclecticism, between 1865 and 1930, the entire gamut of historical styles was revived at one point or another. In many cases, the style was chosen to signify the allegiances or aspirations of the homeowner. The castle built in 1885 for the Chicago hotel impresario Potter Palmer, for example, was clearly intended to identify him as a mercantile prince.

Architecture is an expressive art that creates both physical and psychological effects. While many of its physical features have gone from stone-age to space-age technologies, definitions of architectural beauty have undergone equally radical changes. The history of building styles is intertwined with the

Right: McKim, Mead, and White, Judson Memorial Church (1888–93), Washington Square South, New York. The doorway has Classical columns and a Roman arch in the style of the Italian Renaissance.

Right: Richard E. Schmidt and Hugh E. Garden, Madlener House (1902), Chicago. The doorway reveals the cubic form and exquisite detailing of this Prairie-style house.

changing values of society. When making a conscious choice, Americans have tended to associate their own values with different architectural styles. Thomas Jefferson believed that Classical architecture promoted clear thinking and civic virtues and, thus, was the style best suited for the new republic. The exotic styles of the Middle East, Africa, and Asia appealed to the Victorians, whose globe-trotting spirit of adventure led to explorations of these far-off lands. By the end of the nineteenth century, Frank Lloyd Wright, a son of the Great Plains, argued that European styles were divorced from the American spirit. Wright's new Prairie style was the country's first indigenous architectural style—albeit bearing clear traces of Japanese design influence—since the days of Native Americans.

In the early twentieth century, Modernists wiped the slate clean of historic details and introduced spare new designs based on architectural structure and functionalism. They believed that borrowing styles from European sources was inauthentic and argued for a complete break with the past. The very concept of style was considered obsolete, an outdated vestige that paled by comparison

to the "scientific" method of Modernism. In the latter part of the twentieth century, Post-Modernists challenged that idea and began to use historical features once again, transforming them into sophisticated reinterpretations.

Like their nineteenth-century predecessors, many Americans today are fascinated with historical revivals. These styles have reached a new peak of popularity, particularly in new suburban developments where homes are being built with a combination of features from different eras—an Early American roof, Georgian windows, Greek columns, and a Victorian porch in a single house.

Architects have always borrowed freely from different periods, reinventing styles and creating eclectic combinations. The multiplicity of forms, features, and materials can be confusing and challenging to identify. This guide breaks down the process into easily recognizable details and keys them to specific styles and periods throughout America's history.

Left: Skidmore, Owings, and Merrill, Lever House (1952), New York. The understated glass doors are a feature of the International style.

EARLY AMERICAN—17TH CENTURY

The country's first builders, Native Americans, used natural materials and preindustrial techniques that had a minimal impact on nature. Despite their limited materials and tools, they created complex dwellings that were well adapted to the environment. The stone cliff houses and adobe pueblos of the Southwest were multifamily dwellings with thermal protection against the scorching sun and the cold desert nights. The easily demountable tepees of the Great Plains allowed entire tribes to follow the buffalo herds. Spiritual and social ideals also shaped their structures. The corbelled dome of the Navajo hogans echoed the shape of the heavens, and the kiva, a sacred ritual chamber, was an essential part of the Hopi pueblo. The plank houses of the Northwest tribes were decorated with totem poles and other spiritual symbols, and the functional layout of their interiors was based on the clan structures of the social group. When European colonists arrived on the continent, there were many thriving Native American cultures with a rich variety of building traditions. However, these traditions were soon diminished by disease and conquest.

Right: Cliff Houses (1100–1300), Mesa Verde, Colorado. These Native American dwellings are some of America's earliest stone buildings.

The first European settlers in America were not trained architects, and their early buildings were often far inferior to those of the Native Americans. The crude dugouts of the Salem and Plymouth settlements provided only the barest necessary shelter, with little comfort and no privacy. The reality was far removed from later romanticized visions of the colonial settlements.

Contrary to popular belief, the typical colonial home in the seventeenth century was not a log cabin. Swedish colonists introduced the log cabin in Delaware in 1638, but the New Sweden colony was short lived. The log cabin first became a popular symbol of the

Above: Fort Church (c. 1610), Jamestown, Virginia. A reconstruction of the early timber frame and thatched roof church built by the first settlers.

country's pioneering spirit during the presidential election of 1840. Campaign images depicting William Henry Harrison in a log cabin convinced voters that he was a man of the people, although he actually was born on a Virginia plantation. The log cabin's status as an American icon was permanently established with the story of Abraham Lincoln's humble birth and rise to the presidency. While its use increased as settlers moved west in the nineteenth century, other forms of primitive homes, such as sod houses and dugouts, were equally popular, particularly on the Great Plains where timber was in short supply.

Style was not a priority for the early colonists, nor was there any thought of creating a new architecture for the New World. As transplanted Europeans, they built the same kinds of houses and churches they had known in their homelands. Strong regional rivalries were carried from the Old World. In the seventeenth century, each group of colonists sought a foothold: the Spanish in Florida and the Southwest, the British in New England and Virginia, the Dutch in New Amsterdam and the Hudson River valley, the French in Canada and Louisiana, and Swedes and Germans in the Delaware valley. Each group adapted

Above: Clemence-Irons House (c. 1680), Johnston, Rhode Island. The steeply pitched roof, simple door, and small windows of this early colonial house were built in English medieval traditions. Known as a "stone ender," the house is made of wood except for its stone chimney.

its national building traditions to the American environment, which was generally more extreme than the European climate. Their buildings were essentially folk architecture following the vernacular traditions of Britain and continental Europe. Driven by practical needs and craft traditions, vernacular architecture changes very slowly. The houses built in New England in the seventeenth century were much like those built in the Middle Ages.

Although it is usually the most common kind of building, vernacular architecture is also the least likely to be preserved, and therefore is much less familiar today than mansions or government buildings. The simplicity and depth of tradition reflected in these houses, however, made them appealing to later architects such as Frank Lloyd Wright, who sought the roots of American architecture in the nation's first houses.

Since both labor and capital were limited in the New World, the early buildings were simple structures. Even wealthy families lived in houses with only two rooms on the ground floor. Ceilings were low and the original windows were small, made of tiny panes of precious glass. Massive fireplaces in the middle of the house provided both heat and a place for cooking. American building lagged behind the fashions of European architecture. The timber-framed, unpainted houses in New England, for example, were basically farmhouses—a far cry from the elegant Baroque homes built for the wealthy in England at the same time.

EARLY CLASSICAL STYLES—18TH CENTURY

The eighteenth century brought economic growth, cultural consolidation, and stronger ties to European courts. These forces shortened the time lag between the appearance of new European styles and their introduction in America. Trained builders and carpenters came to the New World, along with architecture books from England. In the absence of trained architects, these books were invaluable to the gentleman builders of the era. They were scarce, however. Even one of the largest libraries, the collection of four thousand books amassed by William Byrd II in Virginia, had only twenty-three books specifically on architecture. Thomas Jefferson's great library of nearly seven thousand volumes, which he sold to the Congress in 1815 to form the core of the Library of Congress, included forty-three books on architecture. Skills in drawing and architectural design were considered important parts of a gentleman's education and some of the most notable American houses were built by such enthusiastic amateurs as George Washington and Thomas Jefferson. Until 1797, when Asher Benjamin published *The Country Builders Assistant* in Greenfield, Massachusetts, all books on architecture were imported from Europe.

The colonies on the East Coast became more unified in the eighteenth century, with a more homogeneous architectural style based on British Classicism. American homes began to imitate British country houses and estates. Classical details such as columns, pediments, and porticos began to appear, along with a new emphasis on symmetry. Hipped roofs replaced the steep medieval gables of earlier homes. Homes such as the Isaac Royall House (1733–37/1747–50) in Medford, Massachusetts, were now larger, with higher ceilings and much bigger windows.

Even in New England, houses were no longer built around a massive central fireplace and chimney. Pairs of chimneys moved to the outer walls instead. Although they could not match the elegance and stone building materials of English houses, northern homes became much more stylish. The new urbanity of American housing can be seen in the McPhedris-Warner House (1718–23) in Portsmouth, New Hampshire. Built of brick with a gambrel roof, it is much more sophisticated than the simple wooden saltboxes that came before it. Stone was still a rarity in American building, but an illusion could be created by cutting wide wooden boards to imitate stone.

Above: Isaac Royall House (1733–37/1747–50), Medford, Massachusetts. The owner of the house, a wealthy merchant, enlarged the house twice, each time making it more Classical in the Georgian manner.

Left: McPhedris-Warner House (1718–23), Portsmouth, New Hampshire. One of the earliest brick Georgian houses in New England, this handsome home was an urbane improvement over the plain wooden structures of the seventeenth century.

Some of the more rural adaptations of European design were creative in their own way. William Pierson has described the language of Classicism at Deerfield, Massachusetts, as being spoken with "a thick Yankee accent." Contrary to earlier beliefs, most houses in the eighteenth century were not painted white—a wide variety of colors has been discovered by modern preservationists. Even in rural Deerfield, some houses were painted in pink and blue; others were left unpainted.

GEORGIAN

This highly creative and significant period of architectural design takes its name from four English kings named George: George I (1714–27), George II (1727–60), George III, (1760–1820), and George IV (1820–30). It coincided with the Age of Enlightenment the remarkable period of scientific, philosophical, cultural, and political reawakening. Georgian style ushered in a new age of elegance, purity, and proportion based on the architectural styles of ancient Rome and Greece. The new sense of rationalism and restraint in design was a reaction to the uncontrolled forms and florid ornamentation of the previous Baroque style.

The Georgian period was one of bubbling prosperity in England, thanks in large part to the vast colonizing efforts of the British government. The new dynasty of royal rulers appreciated the opportunity to distance themselves from the excesses of the past and embraced Roman Classical design as an expression of their own nobility. Members of the court followed suit. Traveling to Italy on the "grand tour," the Earl of Burlington, a man of high influence and large wealth, became enamored with the designs of the sixteenth-century Italian architect Andrea Palladio, whose principles were based on the writings of the ancient Roman architect Vitruvius. Burlington published Palladio's writings in England, making them a model for country houses for the British aristocracy, and in time, for the homes of New England merchants and southern planters.

Palladio produced five types of Classical motifs or orders that became the hallmark of Classical design: the Tuscan, Doric, Ionic, Corinthian, and Composite forms. Doorways, porticos, and windows were now flanked by stately columns. Sash windows came into vogue and the three-part Palladian window became a central feature of symmetrical façades.

FEDERALIST

The Georgian style was succeeded by another Classical style strongly influenced by the British architect Robert Adam. Called either the Adam or Federalist style, after the Federalist period of American government, it is a refinement of the Georgian style.

The term "American Federal" reflects the new nation's independence and the penchant of its wealthy families for elegant architecture. At the same time, the Federalist style was pragmatically American in its fresh approach to Classical traditions. Prominent features include Palladian windows, elliptical fanlights, two-story pilasters, and many carefully crafted details in door surrounds and porticos. This period saw the rise of more professional architects, including America's first great architect, Charles Bulfinch, whose graceful Federal designs for brick town houses and churches profoundly changed the cityscape of Boston.

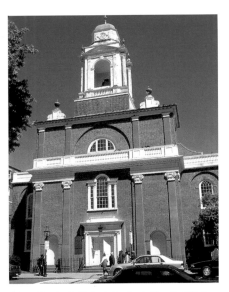

Above: Charles Bulfinch, St. Stephen's Church (1804), Boston. The central Palladian window and symmetry of the façade are characteristic of the Federalist period.

NEOCLASSICAL

Inspired by the archeological excavations at Pompeii and Herculaneum, architects in the late eighteenth and early nineteenth centuries strove for a higher degree of accuracy in the re-creation of ancient forms. The many newly established academies in Europe encouraged artists and architects in this study of history. One of the period's most influential proponents of Classical art, Johann Joachim Winckelmann, summarized the academic attitude: "There is but one way for the moderns to become great, and perhaps unequalled—by imitating the ancients." This did not mean that they were dispassionate; Thomas Jefferson, the most important Neoclassicist in America, described his feelings about a Roman temple he had seen in France as like those of a lover staring at his mistress. This was a romantic Classicism, motivated by high ideals and a yearning for a new and better era.

Jefferson believed that the new republic needed good examples in architecture as well as in politics. Eager to cast off the British implications of Georgian design, he turned to original Greek and Roman models. Although designs were merely copied from ancient prototypes, the rationalist admiration for geometry inspired architects to adopt a style of simplicity and purity of form. Compared to Baroque and Georgian architecture, the Neoclassical style was more severe, with simple colonnades and more planar wall surfaces. It also introduced such other Roman features as domes, stately colonnades, balustrades, loggias, and terraces.

Classical architecture was associated with the foundation of learning and law, and became the preferred style for American libraries and government buildings. Thomas Jefferson's designs for the Virginia State Capitol, the University of Virginia Library, and his home, Monticello (1769–1809) were the first Neoclassical buildings in America. Initially, Jefferson's designs for Monticello were closely modeled on the villas of Andrea Palladio, but the house became increasingly complex as Jefferson transformed the rigid symmetry of the original geometric plan into a

Above: Thomas Jefferson, Monticello (1769–1809), near Charlottesville, Virginia. Jefferson chose Classical forms to connect America to the nobility of republican Rome.

series of rooms shaped by functional requirements and his own personal predilections. Its location on the top of a small mountain echoed the practice of ancient Roman villas, which provided an ideal escape from the city. Other southern mansions were more typically located on lowlands near rivers to take advantage of the ease of transport. Building was a passion for Jefferson. Like many modern home-owners, he never stopped building his ideal house and kept construction going throughout his life.

HISTORIC REVIVALS—PRE CIVIL WAR

In the eclectic nineteenth century, nearly every style that had flourished in European history was revived in American architecture. The new styles came from many parts of Europe, and some came from the Middle East. They were no longer adopted through cultural ties, but were now a matter of deliberate choice, made with a sophisticated awareness of the connection between style and social values. Since trained architects were still rare in the first half of the century—America did not have a school of architecture until 1868—many of the styles were popularized through the publication of pattern books and copied by local builders.

GREEK REVIVAL—1820-1850

The enormous popularity of the Greek Revival made it the first national style in America. It coincided with the spirit of the time, which identified the world of ancient Greece with democratic ideals and the newly independent United States. Architects and builders spread the style across the country, leaving its elegant mark on countless banks, courthouses, homes, and houses of worship, from New England churches and universities to southern plantations and modest cabins. The zenith of the style was reached around 1830 when the Greek façade of a triangular pediment and carefully proportioned columns dominated both public and private buildings. The most remarkable examples were built in Washington, D.C., and the Philadelphia area. Jefferson had supervised the building of the United States Capitol in the Classical style and sponsored its major architect, Benjamin Latrobe.

Right: Henry Howard, Madewood Plantation (1846), Napoleonville, Louisiana. The portico is based on the ancient model of a Greek hexastyle (six-column) temple. The balcony railing is a regional addition characteristic of Louisiana.

Below: Congregational Church (1840s, Slatersville, Rhode Island. The prominent columns and pediment are classic features of a Greek temple.

The interest in ancient Greece was sparked by archeological excavations and the transfer of Greek treasures to European museums, in particular Lord Elgin's removal of the famous sculptures of the Parthenon to London's British Museum in 1801. The political ferment of the War of Independence in Greece between 1821 and 1829 aroused great support in other countries. The poet Lord Byron died fighting for the Greek cause in 1824 and his enormously popular works heightened the craze for all things Greek.

In its simplest form, a Greek Revival home could be built by any carpenter using widely available books with blueprints of Greek temples. One of the most influential was by Asher Benjamin, author of *The American Builder's Companion,* the foremost guide to Greek Revivalism. Traditional pitched roof houses easily accom-

modated the style with the gable end framed by a pediment. The Congregational Church (1840) in Rhode Island is a more careful copy of a Greek portico with four Doric columns. A more elaborate example is Madewood Plantation (1846) in Louisiana, with six graceful Ionic columns across its front.

GOTHIC REVIVAL — 1820–60

This was the first widespread style in America to break away from Classical forms. Based on medieval churches, it was directly linked to Christianity and made its greatest impact on religious buildings. A fervent advocate of Gothic Revival, the British architect Augustus Welby Pugin (1812–1852) maintained that it was the only appropriate style for Christian nations. Pugin's drawings of medieval English churches were models for many American churches, including Trinity Church in New York City (1839–46).

But Gothic Revival also had a strong secular appeal and its characteristic features—arched windows and doors, elaborate towers, medieval masonry, and at times even gargoyles—also found their way to many public buildings and homes. An early example of Gothic Revival architecture is Sunnyside, the home of the writer Washington Irving, in Tarrytown, New York. This was a remodeled Dutch colonial house of the seventeenth century with characteristic stepped gables. The additions included Gothic pointed windows and an expansive porch to allow contact with nature. Popular novels of the day presented an exotic and imaginative view of the Middle Ages that appealed to a wide social spectrum. Whether one lived in a "Carpenter's Gothic" cottage with peaked roofs and gingerbread trim, or a grand villa with towers and pinnacles like Lyndhurst (1838–65), in Tarrytown, New York, the Gothic style offered Americans the sense of a romantic, medieval past. Pattern books such as Andrew Jackson Downing's *Cottage Residences* (1842) described Gothic homes as signs of individuality and sophistication. In contrast to the studied symmetry of Greek Revival, the picturesque, irregular forms of Gothic architecture were thought to be more accurate reflections of the natural world.

Even Frank Lloyd Wright identified the Gothic spirit with a true apprehension of natural principles and harmony with nature, which he called organic architecture. In 1910, Wright asserted in the introduction to the first German publication of his works that the feeling for the organic quality of form was more perfectly realized in Gothic architecture than in any other style.

Left: Brooks House (1851), Salem, Massachusetts. Picturesque Gothic Revival cottages like this one were closely copied from architectural pattern books of the mid-nineteenth century.

Below: Alexander Jackson Davis, Lyndhurst (1838–65), Tarrytown, New York. The irregular forms and large porches of Gothic Revival mansions were considered to be closely attuned to nature.

Nostalgia for the richness of European cultural life was also a factor in the popularity of the Gothic style. The Wedding Cake House (1855), built by George Bourne in Kennebunkport, Maine, is an ornate refashioning of a plain Federalist box into a dazzling display of the carpenter's prowess with a scroll saw that was intended to suggest the style of Milan Cathedral.

The appeal of medieval architecture resonated powerfully in a society that believed one's home is one's castle. One of the grandest of nineteenth-century houses was built for Potter and Berthe Palmer in Chicago, between 1883 and 1885. This castle provided an appropriate setting for the Palmers' art collection, which would later form the core of the Impressionist paintings at the Chicago Art Institute. Their palatial home provided a symbolic link between the new mercantile royalty of Chicago and the aristocratic traditions of the Old World. Medieval castles for urban merchants and suburban squires were built fairly frequently between 1840 and 1940. The home of the Shakespearean actor Edwin Forrest, Fonthill (1848), was a dramatic example built in the Bronx, New York.

Above: Swiss cottage (c. 1860), Tolland, Connecticut. The Swiss cottage mode was characterized by wide overhanging eaves, ornate gingerbread woodwork, and often a large balcony projecting from the second story.

SWISS CHALET

The Swiss Chalet style appealed to those with a taste for the picturesque and nostalgia for European mountain settings. Like many other historical styles of this period, it was introduced into America by Andrew Jackson Downing's pattern books. While Downing stressed the importance of an appropriately romantic site—bold and mountainous if possible—Swiss Chalet–style homes were often built in suburban areas. In 1858, Samuel Colt built a whole neighborhood of Swiss-style cottages for German workers in his wicker factory in Hartford, Connecticut. The area, near Colt's firearms factory, was known as "Little Potsdam." Rough-cut wood was the style's essential building material. Wide overhanging eaves, ornate gingerbread trim, and large balconies were the characteristic features. In the second half of the twentieth century, the Swiss villa was revived as a favorite style for housing developments near ski resorts.

COMMUNITARIAN HOUSING

Experiments in utopian or idealistic living form a constant thread in American culture. Some of these brought interesting architectural possibilities, although only the religious groups such as the Shakers actually developed long-lasting communities. Robert Owen, a British industrialist with progressive ideals, proposed a European-style communal development at New Harmony, Indiana. This communal center for work and social activities was designed by Steadman Whitwell in 1825, but was never built. The desire to create a new and reformed mode of living had motivated the early Puritans, as well as such

Left: The Cloisters (1743), Ephrata, Pennsylvania. These residences were built by an idealistic and celibate religious community. The simple, medieval style was a deliberate choice at a time when American architecture was following more stylish Classical fashions.

worldly idealists as Thomas Jefferson. Even such idiosyncratic examples as Henry David Thoreau's simple cabin at Walden Pond (1847) reflect a philosophical return to simplicity. Thoreau built the cabin himself to re-create the essence of frontier life—within walking distance of the quite civilized center of Concord, Massachusetts.

Reformers paid attention to the individual family home as well. Catharine Beecher and her well-known sister, Harriet Beecher Stowe, attempted to reform domestic architecture, paying particular attention to the actual patterns of work within the household. Catharine Beecher published her *Treatise on Domestic Economy* in 1841, and *The American Woman's Home* with her sister in 1869. The external form of the house in these books remained conventional—the innovations were inside. Catharine Beecher's designs incorporated technological improvements in heating and plumbing to enhance health and relieve the burden of the women, who did most of the work. Laundry and kitchen areas were reorganized for convenience. Although servants were still commonly employed at this time—in 1850 Andrew Jackson Downing defined a cottage as any house with less than three servants—both Downing and Beecher agreed that servants would become less common as other economic opportunities arose, and that houses would have to become more efficient to save domestic labor.

INDUSTRIAL WORKERS HOUSING

The pragmatic counterpart to idealistic communitarian developments was the low-cost housing built for workers after the Industrial Revolution. Housing for workers was an urgent need in the nineteenth century, a time of rising capitalism and large factories. Many examples of worker housing still survive in the New England area. The Boott Mill Complex in Lowell (begun 1821) included dormitories and row houses for mill workers. New England was tapping a new labor source—thousands of single women who left farms for the first time to work in the factories. Some surviving examples of mill towns, such as Harrisville, New Hampshire (built 1820–60), provide examples of smaller-scale worker housing, with rows of identical small houses. The streetcar suburbs of Dorchester and Jamaica Plain, Massachusetts, became urbanized with block after block of triple deckers—houses with homes on three floors for separate families.

Above: Worker housing at Lowell, Massachusetts. In the first half of the nineteenth century, new cotton and wool mills created a need to house large numbers of workers. Lowell innovated boarding houses for single women who were entering the industrial workforce for the first time.

OCTAGON HOUSES

Eight-sided houses were promoted as healthful alternatives by Orson Squire Fowler, a popular phrenologist of the day. Phrenology was a nineteenth-century belief that mental, and even moral, faculties could be revealed by studying external bumps on the skull. Fowler's claims for octagon houses, however, were based on more discernible qualities. As maintained in his 1849 pattern book, the houses offered maximum light, space, and ventilation by eliminating "dark and useless corners." Besides touting the efficiency of the octagonal plan, Fowler's book urged the use of concrete for solid foundations and healthful basements. This was one of the earliest uses of concrete in American architecture. The book was a great success and led to the construction of many octagon houses across the country, most commonly in New York, New England, and the Midwest. However, the octagon shape had disadvantages, in particular, awkwardly shaped interior rooms. Few of the original houses survive today.

Right: Octagon House (1857), Richmond, Rhode Island. Eight-sided homes like this one were promoted as healthy dwellings that eliminated "dark and useless corners." Although many octagon houses were built in the mid-nineteenth century, the shape created awkward room layouts, and few of these homes survive today.

Far right: Italianate villa, Hartford, Connecticut. The flat roofline and overhanging eaves are characteristic of the Italianate style.

ITALIANATE — 1850-70

The Italianate style brought the romance of Italian villas within reach of American homeowners. Like the Gothic Revival, it had broad appeal and could be adapted easily to both wood-frame structures and stone villas. It was a distinctive style with flat roofs and overhanging eaves, often ornamented by elaborate brackets. Pattern books offered various choices, a cubic form or an L-shaped plan with an asymmetrically placed tower, and promoted the style for those with artistic tastes.

EGYPTIAN REVIVAL—1840-60

The nineteenth century was a time of fascination with exotic places. The Egyptian Revival had a strong impact on the design of public memorials, from the Washington Monument (1848–85) to cemetery monuments and gates. It also appeared in some houses and churches, notably Minard Lafever's First Presbyterian Church in Sag Harbor, New York. Built in 1844, it has sloping walls in an Egyptian pylon shape. The style faded after 1860, but Egyptomania was resurrected in the 1920s and exerted a strong influence on the Art Deco style.

Right: Minard Lafever, First Presbyterian Church (1843), Sag Harbor, New York. A rare and important example of the Egyptian Revival style. The sloping walls of the entrance resemble Egyptian pylons.

Far right: Richard Upjohn, Old St. Paul's Episcopal Church (1856), Baltimore, Maryland. This Early Romanesque church has the rounded arches, long narrow windows, and solid masonry of early medieval architecture.

EARLY ROMANESQUE REVIVAL—1844-70

The earmarks of this style are rounded arches, frequently grouped together in arcades, and thick walls and narrow windows, all derived from European Romanesque architecture of the early Middle Ages. Richard Upjohn's Old St. Paul's Church in Baltimore (1856) is an excellent example.

HIGH VICTORIAN—POST CIVIL WAR

The term *Victorian* is used on both sides of the Atlantic to define the span of Queen Victoria's reign from 1837 to 1901. While Greek and Gothic Revivals dominated the first part of her reign, it is the last forty years of wildly eclectic, highly decorated styles that are considered High Victorian, particularly in American architecture. This post–Civil War age was one of economic and geographic expansion in the United States, fueled by major advances in industrialization and the rapid growth of the railroads. Mass production made it possible for retailers to offer complex designs in roofs, doors, windows and other building features to a much wider market than just wealthy households. The railroads transported the materials at relatively low cost, spreading the elaborate detailing of High Victorian styles to homes, churches, and civic buildings across the country.

New construction moved at a furious pace with the new balloon frames made of lightweight, machine-cut lumber and nails. This technique replaced the much slower method of post-and-beam or mortise-and-tenon construction. With cheap lumber and nails, a father and son could now frame a house in the time that it once took twenty men to complete it the old-fashioned way.

But this was also the age of iron and steel, leading to new challenges on how buildings could be constructed and how high they could reach. Wonders in engineering, such as the construction of the Brooklyn Bridge from 1869 to 1883, symbolized the unprecedented achievements of the era.

While iron bridges demonstrated a new ability to harness nature, steam engines and railroads allowed people to travel to places they had only imagined in the past. The expansion of the British Empire through Africa, India, the Far East, Middle East, and the islands of the Caribbean and the Pacific put the Western world in touch with exotic cultures and building styles. The profile of a single block in a late-nineteenth-century American town could include a mélange of features from the far reaches of the globe—a home with a French mansard roof standing next to one with Moorish Revival turrets.

Above all else, diversity and eclecticism prevailed. Although styles were still largely derived from European precedent, increasingly signs of innovation began to appear. In addition a new professionalism emerged at this time, with the first school of architecture founded at the Massachusetts

Institute of Technology in 1868. Illustrated journals of architecture also appeared in the 1880s. Industrialization created a new moneyed class with the means to build impressive new homes. High Victorian houses were large and typically had a variety of rooms dedicated to special purposes such as parlor, library, nursery, sewing room, dining room, and breakfast room. Rooms, if not form, followed function. The proliferation of specialized spaces represented a dramatic departure from the seventeenth-century and even eighteenth-century houses, where a single room served many different purposes. New concepts of private life also flourished at this time. The novels of Henry James and the development of psychoanalysis at the turn of the century present a cultural parallel to the new architectural designs. With their picturesque irregularity and many inner spaces, Victorian homes literally reflected a more complex view of the self. Perhaps this is why psychological thrillers, from Henry James's *Turn of the Screw* to the films of Alfred Hitchcock are often set in Victorian houses. Norman Bates's Second Empire Baroque house in *Psycho* (1960) is a prime example.

Left: Calvert Vaux and Frederic Church, Olana (1870), near Hudson, New York. This High Victorian mansion, built for the landscape painter Frederic Church, reflects his fascination with colorful, exotic places. Derived from Arabic, the name Olana means 'Our place on high."

HIGH VICTORIAN OR RUSKINIAN GOTHIC — 1860–80

While the earlier Gothic Revival style was based on English medieval models, High Victorian Gothic was a more vibrant style drawn from northern Italy and France. It was inspired by the writings of the British art critic John Ruskin. His emphasis on the colorful, patterned masonry and irregular forms of Venetian and French Gothic architecture is called Ruskinian Gothic. It was one of the dominant styles for public buildings during this period. Although its extravagant form was used less often for residences, several remarkable exceptions still stand. Olana, the richly eclectic house built for the painter Frederick Church in 1870 is in a class by itself. This towered mansion in upstate New York incorporates Islamic arches and Chinese tiles, tokens of Church's passion for travel, in a dramatically picturesque setting overlooking the Hudson River. Mark Twain's remarkable house in Hartford, Connecticut, designed by Edward Potter in 1874, is equally striking. A large, rambling structure with many gables, porches, and sculptural chimneys, Twain's house uses combinations of colored bricks to create a vibrant polychromatic effect.

SECOND EMPIRE — 1860–70

The hallmark feature of this style is the distinctive profile of the mansard roof. The style is named for the period when it began, in France's Second Empire of Napoleon III. Prince Louis Napoleon, nephew of the French emperor, became the new emperor in 1852 and, for the next two decades, reshaped the city of Paris in the new style. Much of what the world knows today as the elegant cityscape of boulevards in the French capital was redesigned under Napoleon III's influence. The grandeur of this period of French architecture, a richly expressive style of tall buildings, steep, double-sided mansard roofs, multiple windows, Classical pediments, and imposing balconies, is notably expressed in showcase buildings such as the Paris Opera House and in the expansion of the Louvre.

Although Napoleon III ended his days in exile after France's disastrous defeat by Germany in the Franco-Prussian War in 1870, by then the Second Empire style had taken firm root in other countries. The Paris Exhibitions of 1855 and 1867 had popularized the style in England. But as popular as it was

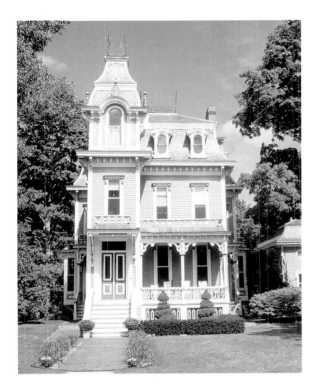

*Left: George Lord Little House
(1875), Kennebunkport, Maine.
The mansard roof is the hallmark
of the Second Empire style. It
originated in France and was
a popular choice for American
homes and government buildings
in the 1860s and 1870s.*

in Europe, nothing could match its overwhelming reception in America. Denoting authority and Classical elegance, the Second Empire style perfectly fit America's sense of growing national pride in its prosperity in the period following the Civil War. The Old Executive Office Building in Washington, D.C., Philadelphia's City Hall, and New York State's Capitol were all built in the Second Empire style. So many Second Empire buildings were constructed during the presidency of Ulysses S. Grant (1869–77) that the style was often called the "General Grant style." Considered progressive and modern, it also became a highly popular style in domestic architecture. Particularly in the northeast, Second Empire homes were best sellers. The familiar mansard roof transformed the character of many small towns and became the quintessential expression of American aspiration. It was so popular that it seemed to be an American original. With machine-made details, Second Empire homes were often richly embellished. Large wraparound porches permitted family members and neighbors to socialize in large-scale comfort. Ironically, when many of these large homes fell into disrepair, their exuberant Gothic qualities lent themselves to countless tales of fright and horror as the perfect setting for haunted terror.

STICK STYLE—1860-90

The High Victorian passion for ornament and individualism, combined with America's thriving lumber industry, led to the creation of this highly decorated style of wooden architecture. It featured angular and rectilinear patterns of boards used as ornament on home exteriors. It grew from the Picturesque Gothic style first popularized by Alexander Jackson Davis and Andrew Jackson Downing in such publi-

Right: Richard Morris Hunt, John Griswold House (1863), Newport, Rhode Island. One of the earliest and finest examples of the High Victorian Stick style.

cations as Davis's *Rural Residences (1837)* and Dowring's *The Architecture of Country Houses* (1850). It was further developed in the pattern books of the 1860s and 1870s. The invention of the balloon frame and the steam-powered scroll saw made wood the preferred material of construction, especially as lumber was in plentiful supply in many areas and was both cheaper and less difficult to work with than stone. The Stick style is generally considered to be a link between the Gothic Revival and Queen Anne styles. Although it was quickly supplanted in the Northeast by the widely popular Queen Anne style, it reached a distinctive expression in San Francisco. From the Gold Rush period forward, the city expanded with many Stick-style houses built from the plentiful supplies of redwood. Many of the finest surviving examples are the colorfully painted, multistoried houses known as the "Painted Ladies."

QUEEN ANNE — 1880–1910

The epitome of a Victorian house to many people, the Queen Anne style was the culmination of all Victorian styles in its eclectic mix of features: gingerbread trim, turrets, large wooden porches, and spindlework. Above all else, its defining feature was decorative detailing in an exuberant mix of color, often with wooden appliqué in sunflower or sunburst forms. Viewed as a symbol of life and creativity, the sunflower was used in many forms, including ceramic decoration, metalwork, and stucco. Queen Anne houses also used swags and Roman garland appliqués, along with tinted and stained-glass windows. Like Shingle-style homes popular at the same time, Queen Anne houses frequently had shingled siding and roofs; however, the Queen Anne style has much more detailing and color.

The style originated in England in the 1870s but had little to do with the much earlier reign of Queen Anne (1702–14). It borrowed heavily from the preceding Tudor and Stuart eras, using brick and stucco, elaborate gables, half timbering, and a variety of window forms. The Queen Anne style received wide coverage in America at the Philadelphia Centennial of 1876, quickly supplanting the two most popular contemporary styles, Second Empire and Gothic. Its chief rival, the Romanesque style, was essentially stone-built, putting it beyond the means of most Americans. Ease of construction and economies of building meant that wooden Queen Anne houses could be erected by competent carpenters using widely circulated pattern books for every detail from intricate exterior detailing to a maze of interior rooms. As a result, Queen Anne houses throughout the country show few regional differences. By the 1890s, homes built in this eclectic style even began to incorporate Classical components, such as Palladian windows.

The second half of the nineteenth century saw a marked increase in leisure time for the middle class and the creation of new resorts. The seaside resort town of Cape May, New Jersey, was one of the first. After a series of devastating fires, it was rebuilt about 1870 and today is still a showcase of ornate Victorian homes. The wealthiest individuals also built conspicuously magnificent summer mansions near the sea. The highest concentration of these gilded-era mansions, many of which rival European palaces, was built in Newport, Rhode Island.

Right: Queen Anne house, Jamaica Plain, Massachusetts. This High Victorian style is marked by decorative detailing and an exuberant mix of color and wooden appliqué.

Far right: William Mead and Stanford White, Isaac Bell House (1883), Newport, Rhode Island. Shingle-style homes and churches were wrapped in a continuous skin of shingles that unified their irregular form.

SHINGLE STYLE — 1875–1900

The Shingle style was one of the first styles to tap into American building history. Partly inspired by seventeenth-century colonial architecture when many houses were covered with shingles instead of clapboards, this style also included design elements from Japan and from Britain. The centennial exhibition of 1876, commemorating the Declaration of Independence, helped encourage interest in American design precedents. Architects such as Stanford White and Charles McKim made sketching tours of New England villages and published some of their drawings. Their house for Isaac Bell (1881–83) in Newport, Rhode Island, is one of the most impressive Shingle-style houses. Henry Hobson Richardson also used this style to great effect, and the earliest work of Frank Lloyd Wright, including his own house in Oak Park in 1889, was built in the Shingle style.

The distinguishing feature of this style is a continuous skin of wooden shingles on the roof, sometimes continuing on exterior walls. Although these homes often had broad turrets and large porches, the shingles unified the design and offered an alternative to the busy variety of materials and forms in Queen Anne and Stick styles. The style originated when Richardson of Boston and McKim, Mead, and White of New York began to build summer houses for wealthy clients in the New England seaside resorts of Cape Cod, Newport, and coastal Maine in the 1870s. Many of these homes survive today, along with scattered examples of the style built well into the first decade of the twentieth century in other regions. Porches, a marked feature of other Victorian houses, often completely surround coastal Shingle houses to take advantage of the sea air. The form also borrowed features from other eras, such as Classical columns and gambrel roofs from New England colonial designs.

Right: Henry Hobson Richardson, Stonehurst, Robert Treat Paine House (1884–86), Waltham, Massachusetts. A noted example of the Shingle style. Richardson updated a Second Empire mansard house with large additions including a sweeping porch and a continuous skin of shingles, combined with a rugged masonry base. The second-story Palladian window is a carryover from the Georgian style of the previous century.

Richardson's design for Stonehurst, the Robert Treat Paine House (1884–86) is a premier example of the Shingle style. Working with Frederick Law Olmsted, the principal designer of New York City's Central Park, Richardson chose glacial boulders drawn from the site as a major design feature. The first floor is clad in these boulders and a shingled first-floor loggia rises above a porch constructed from bouldered piers. The seamless qualities of the Shingle style can be seen at their most dramatic here—the cladding is unbroken by decorative detail of any sort, so that the play of light over stone and shingle surfaces produces a unique effect.

Above: Henry Hobson Richardson, Trinity Church (1872–77), Boston. The first major American architect to develop a distinctly personal style, Richardson used Romanesque features in highly original designs.

RICHARDSONIAN ROMANESQUE— 1870-95

Henry Hobson Richardson's signature style of rugged stonework was so distinctive that it became identified with a unique style that bears his name. Richardson adapted the heavy stone construction of French and Spanish Romanesque architecture, notably the massive, semicircular arch that became known as the Richardsonian arch. He also used masonry in artful combinations of colors, patterns, and textures, as in his masterpiece, Trinity Church in Boston. Although Richardson died young, his style was carried on by others in this period and influenced the later work of major architects such as Louis Sullivan.

FOLK VICTORIAN—1870-1910

In addition to architect-designed buildings, carpenters and builders in this period displayed their own highly creative expression of the High Victorian style. Folk Victorian houses, like so many built in the nineteenth century, were typically constructed with a balloon frame. But they often incorporated an eclectic mix of styles, including Gothic Revival and Italianate features. The style was most prevalent after the coming of the railroad up to just before World War I. Examples can be found all across the country.

ODDITIES

Delightfully odd houses were also built during the late Victorian period. One of the most unusual was "Lucy," the house built in the shape of an elephant in Margate, New Jersey. Patented by James Lafferty in 1881, this house was made of a wooden frame covered with tin and painted to look like a real elephant. It had two floors of living space inside the body of the elephant, and a belvedere for viewing the seascape built in the shape of a howdah (riding platform) on the elephant's back. The staircase was in a rear leg. Although built for publicity purposes, this structure perhaps carried the metaphor of natural shapes for houses a bit too far. Only three of these houses were built, and only Lucy remains. After serving as a house, tavern, and hotel, it is now a museum.

Left: James Lafferty, "Lucy" elephant house (1881), Margate, New Jersey. Built as a publicity stunt, this odd structure of wood covered with tin was actually used as a house, with the staircase in a rear leg. It later became a tavern and hotel, and is now a museum.

Far left: Folk Victorian house, Haddam, Connecticut. A striking mixture of styles, including a Greek Revival gable, Renaissance arches on the porch and windows, and a Second Empire tower and cupola.

MOORISH REVIVAL — 1870s–1900

A number of elaborate houses of worship were built in the late nineteenth century in styles reflecting the cultural origins of their congregations. The Moorish Revival was used especially for synagogues to reflect the golden age of Judaism in Spain during Muslim rule. Highly detailed Flemish, Northern Baroque, Russian Orthodox, and Spanish Colonial churches also were built in this period for specific ethnic groups.

Right: Henry Fernbach, Central Synagogue (1872), New York. Built by the first Jewish architect in America, this synagogue has many features of the Moorish Revival style, including domed towers and horseshoe arches over the doorway and windows. The distinctive rose window is a geometric design based on Islamic patterns.

REVIVALS AND RADICAL CHANGES— 1890s TO WORLD WAR II

Greek and Roman Classical styles came back with a bang after the World's Columbian Exposition of 1893 in Chicago. Called the White City, the fairgrounds were an enormous showcase of grand Classical structures and led to a new wave of imposing columns, porticos and other Classical details in buildings throughout the country. Many architects now had extensive academic training, and the revivals were frequently more historically accurate than in the preceding decades. A number of other historic styles were introduced from England, France, and Italy, complete with the new standards of comfort—central heating, plumbing, and electricity.

The United States took a leading role in architecture after the great Chicago fire of 1871. The ensuing building boom instigated the greatest rethinking of city architecture in history. New building techniques and technologies allowed forward-thinking architects such as the Chicago-based firm of Adler and Sullivan to devise the skyscraper. This new, uniquely American style influenced the rest of the world. From the late nineteenth century onward, buildings reached new heights in ever more extravagant and daring designs, occasionally harking back to historical precedent but increasingly exploring original forms. But this would be a time of much bigger changes. As the Industrial Revolution progressed, urban populations began to explode. Boston went from a population of about 15,000 at the time of the American Revolution to over a half million by 1900. Chicago grew from a population of less than 30,000 in 1850 to nearly 1.7 million by the end of the century. Suburbs also grew at a tremendous pace, made possible by the development of streetcars and, later, subways.

In reaction to this overwhelming industrialization and urban growth, many people developed a new appreciation for the religious and social values of the Middle Ages. William Morris and John Ruskin in England promoted the idea that a return to handcrafted medieval arts would provide an antidote to the alienation of modern industrial society. The Arts and Crafts movement that they inspired was enthusiastically received in the United States. A large number of homes were designed by American followers of this movement from about 1880 through the 1920s. From 1901 to 1916, Gustav Stickley, a noted furniture maker, published *The Craftsman*, a magazine with photographs and plans of homes and furniture embodying the principles of the Arts and Crafts movement. Frank Lloyd Wright shared many of these values. In 1901, he lectured at Hull House in Chicago on "The Art and Craft of the Machine." In this lecture he defined some of the principles of his new Prairie-style homes, arguing for the artistic use of machinery and mass production, rather than a return to strict medieval craftsmanship.

After World War I, homes built in the Colonial Revival and other traditional styles still dominated the housing market, but new Modernist experiments emerged, especially in California. Architects in Europe embraced the modern materials of metal and glass, and firmly rejected historical ornament. Many of them admired and were influenced by Frank Lloyd Wright, but they went even further in creating a new style for the new age. These Modernist styles at first appealed only to a small elite seeking a new mode of life, but eventually were embraced by a broader segment of American society. At first, as Michael Webb has observed, the American public was as "shocked by nudity in buildings as in people." However, the focus on the modern resonated with the longstanding American desire to create a new world, beyond Europe's borders, owing nothing to the past.

BEAUX ARTS — 1885–1930

This style takes its name from the Ecole des Beaux-Arts in Paris, the premiere architecture school of the day, where American architects learned the language of Classicism. Although Chicago had its own style, established by Louis Sullivan, Frank Lloyd Wright, and other original talents, the city's leaders passed them by and chose prestigious Beaux Arts architects to design the World's Columbian Exposition. Led by the prominent architectural firm of McKim, Mead, and White of New York City, the Beaux Arts style—formal, symmetrical, and lavishly ornamented with Classical details—dominated the fair and the shape of American architecture for decades to come. It shaped imposing public buildings such as the United States Customs House (1899–1907) and Grand Central Station (1903–13) in New York City, and formal homes such as Nemours (1910), the Du Pont estate in Delaware.

Above: Carrere and Hastings, Nemours (1910), the Alfred I. Du Pont estate, Wilmington, Delaware. The Classical formality of the Beaux Arts style was an unmistakable sign of the great wealth and power of families such as the Du Ponts.

NEOCLASSICAL REVIVAL — 1895-1950

Although the World's Columbian Exposition also led to the Neoclassical Revival, this style was less formal than the Beaux Arts and could be adapted to both expensive and modest homes.

TUDOR—1890–1940

The Tudor style is among the most highly romantic and picturesque of the vernacular revival styles. Like other revivals of the late nineteenth century, it was part of a design trend toward greater accuracy in the use of source materials. While it was based on new interpretations of late-medieval English vernacular forms, it incorporated the latest in modern materials. Both simple cottages and lavish mansions imitated the English Tudor style of steeply pitched roofs and half-timbered façades. Decorative ornamentation, especially around entry porches and windows, drew from more eclectic sources, including the Italian Renaissance and the Arts and Crafts movement. The Tudor Revival style became extremely fashionable for both large and small American homes in the 1920s and 1930s when complete building kits became available through Sears and other mail-order catalogs. Although it faded around World War I, Tudor Revival reappeared in the 1970s and has remained a popular, much simplified suburban house style.

Left: Tudor-style house (1920s), Newton, Massachusetts. The Tudor style was highly fashionable in the 1920s and 1930s for both large and small American homes. It faded just before World War II and reappeared again in the mid-1970s.

Far left: T. M. Russell House (1902), Middletown, Connecticut. The Neoclassical Revival style is less formal than the Beaux Arts. While the scale of the double-height columns suits this large home, it also was often reduced to fit more modest housing.

CHÂTEAUESQUE—
1880–1910

Richard Morris Hunt, the first American to graduate from the Ecole des Beaux-Arts in Paris, introduced the Châteauesque style. Inspired by French châteaux, the style was used in a wide range of houses from sumptuous estates and city mansions, such as those Hunt designed for the Vanderbilt family, to wood or brick suburban homes. The chief characteristics are sharply pitched and hipped roofs with conical towers.

Above right: Cass Gilbert, Isaac Fletcher House (1899), New York. This urban mansion displays the flamboyant features of the Châteauesque style.

Right: Châteauesque house (1890s), Newton, Massachusetts. Suburban homes imitated the style of French châteaux by substituting wood for expensive white limestone.

FRENCH ECLECTIC — 1918–45

In contrast to the French château, this style was based on the less pretentious farm buildings and manor houses of rural France, particularly of Normandy and Brittany. The details were rich and varied, but generally included fortresslike masonry walls, steeply hipped roofs, round towers, and massive chimneys. Photography books of these French buildings circulated in America after World War I. Equally important, thousands of American servicemen came back from France after the war with poignant memories of these picturesque country homes.

Left: Frederick J. Sterner, Falaise (1920s), Long Island, New York. An important landmark of the French Eclectic style, this grand country house was designed for Harry Guggenheim, a gentleman of Francophile tastes who served in France during World War I. It is based on rural manor homes in Normandy.

ITALIAN RENAISSANCE—1890-1937

This is the style that created some of the most elaborate Italian Renaissance villas in America: San Simeon, the Hearst Mansion in California (1937), the Villard Houses in New York City (1883), and Vizcaya in Miami (1916). Much simpler, suburban versions were built in the 1920s with the characteristic Mediterranean features: tiled, low hipped roofs, rounded arch doorways, and stucco exteriors. Although very similar to Spanish Mission style homes, the overhangs in Italian Renaissance homes are not as broad.

Above: Italian Renaissance Revival house (c. 1920s), Newton, Massachusetts. This was a more accurate representation of Mediterranean homes than the earlier Italianate style.

SPANISH REVIVALS—1890-1955

While French, British, and Italian revivals were spreading across the country, California and the Southwest held on to their Spanish colonial traditions. Despite the unifying force of the new transcontinental railroad, the Spanish colonial tradition continued to be reflected in several revival styles including:

Mission Style—c. 1890-1920 This style originated in California and re-creates the earlier Spanish colonial architecture. Houses feature stucco walls and red tile roofs, with Spanish-inspired detailing. The Mission style gained momentum when the Southern Pacific and Santa Fe railroads adopted the style for its stations throughout the Southwest. The style is characterized not by archeological accuracy but by a somewhat free adaptation of major features drawn from historic models.

Spanish Eclectic—c. 1915-40 More historically accurate than Mission style, Spanish Eclectic incorporates aspects of the entire history of Spanish building. The style was given a major boost from the Panama-California Exposition in San Diego (1915–16), and the contemporary studies of Spanish architecture by Bertram Grosvenor Goodhue, designer of the exhibition. It is most common in the southwestern states and Florida.

Above: Scotty's Castle (1922–29), Death Valley, California. This is an extravagant example of the Spanish Eclectic style, one of several Spanish revivals that started in California. The style became equally popular in Texas and the Southwest as these areas developed in the 1920s and 1930s.

Monterey—c. 1925-55 Most frequently found in California and Texas, Monterey is a mixture of Spanish Eclectic and Eastern Colonial Revival styles.

Pueblo Revival—c. 1910–present Most common in Arizona and New Mexico, Pueblo Revival is a mixture of elements from Spanish adobe flat-roofed construction and Native American pueblos.

However, regionalism was not absolute. Stucco walls, red tile roofs, and even the adobe flat-roof construction of Native American pueblos have found their way back east to homes in Cape May, New Jersey, and New England.

CRAFTSMAN — 1901-30

The roots of the Craftsman style are in the Arts and Crafts movement that began in England in the mid-nineteenth century, a time when many artists and art critics returned to the style of medieval handicrafts as an alternative to increasing mass production in the industrial age. Gustav Stickley's magazine, *The Craftsman* (1901–16), gave the style its name in America. The style was essentially a back-to-basics movement, a rejection of the clutter of High Victorian architecture, and a precursor of Modernism. The Gamble House (1908) in Pasadena, California, by Charles and Henry Greene is a noted example of Craftsman architecture: low roofs, overhanging eaves, exposed rafters, and exquisite detailing. Smaller Craftsman-style bungalows were one of the most popular building formats in the nation. Frank Lloyd Wright would carry the same principles of simplicity and craftsmanship into his highly inventive style.

Right: Greene and Greene, Gamble House (1908), Pasadena, California. Handcrafted and beautifully detailed, both inside and out, the Gamble House is a masterpiece of the Craftsman style. It was one of the first homes adapted for California living with sheltered decks and sleeping porches beyond its exterior walls.

PRAIRIE STYLE—1890s-1920

Frank Lloyd Wright was one of the earliest and strongest proponents of an original American style—and the Prairie house was his answer. The low, horizontal lines echoed the midwestern prairie. The flowing room plans and low ceilings accommodated modern lifestyles. These homes also incorporated the Craftsman qualities of beautifully detailed windows and doors. But unlike Craftsman proponents, Wright and other members of the Prairie school believed that architecture should take advantage of

Above: Frank Lloyd Wright, Willits House (1903), Highland Park, Illinois Dramatically low-lying, rambling, and asymmetrical, this house exemplifies the Prairie style. Wright used the horizontal sweep to create a flowing room plan and to reflect the Midwestern landscape.

machine technology. And while they rejected European precedents, they embraced aspects of Asian design, such as the low roofs and overhanging eaves of Japanese architecture.

Wright's later organic architecture and Usonian houses extended the principles of the Prairie school. Both Wright and Louis Sullivan strongly condemned American architects' continued borrowing of European forms. In his introduction to the edition of his works published in 1910 in Germany, Wright declared that the use of forms borrowed from other stylistic periods and cultures will inevitably lead to an architecture divorced from the inner life of the people. Wright noted that American culture was particularly susceptible to this alienation, since it had no traditional architecture. In an interview with William MacDonald in 1958, Wright explained that he borrowed the term *Usonia* from the English writer Samuel Butler, who used it to replace the more long-winded "United States of America." The word *Usonia* was also linked to the concept of freedom, and, for Wright, the term *Usonian architecture* therefore meant free architecture, "an architecture for democracy."

Wright developed a new concept of space in architecture. Rather than seeing the house as a box containing various rooms, he wanted to create the interiors first, and then shape the house around them. His concept of space was strikingly dynamic and almost mystical, as he explained in *The Future of Architecture* in 1953: "Space. The continual becoming: invisible fountain from which all rhythms flow and to which they must pass. Beyond time or infinity." By emphasizing the flow of space in his houses, Wright helped shift American architecture from an architecture of solid mass to one of volume and transparency. With windows treated as banks of light screens, walls also became more dynamic.

Although Wright's designs are highly individualistic, his influence on modern American architecture is profound. Derivative styles echoing his linear simplicity and bare-bones domestic influence can be seen in suburbs across America. While many of these track housing communities lack the quality and grace that Wright espoused in his Usonian concept for affordable homes, his vision of the need for modern utilitarian design was both inspired and widely imitated. Every American ranch-style house is rooted in Wright's idealism.

MODERNIST OR INTERNATIONAL STYLE— 1925 TO PRESENT

When Ludwig Mies van der Rohe, the leader of the International style in America, said "God is in the details," he was talking about a revolutionary concept of architecture. Along with other Modernist architects, he rejected historical detail as a cover-up for what they believed was the essence of architecture—its internal structure. The materials they used—glass, steel, and exposed concrete—emphasized structural details.

Left: Philip Johnson, Philip Johnson Glass House (1946–49), New Canaan, Connecticut. A showcase for the Modernist or International style, the Glass House abolished the tradition of privacy in favor of progressive design. It also introduced an elegant use of industrial metalwork as an acceptable material for residential architecture.

The International style was named for a 1932 exhibition of the works of Le Corbusier, Ludwig Mies van der Rohe, and Walter Gropius at the Museum of Modern Art in New York City. European-born architects such as Rudolph Schindler and Richard Neutra brought firsthand knowledge of these new directions to America. Significantly, both men came to the United States to work with Frank Lloyd Wright in the early 1920s. Two of the main creators of the International style, Walter Gropius and Mies van der Rohe, emigrated to America in the late 1930s to escape Nazi Germany, which rejected the tenets of Modernism. Both Gropius and Mies had a tremendous effect on American architecture, through their buildings as well as their teaching. Gropius headed the Harvard School of Design, while Mies van der Rohe directed the Illinois Institute of Technology in Chicago. Gropius's home in Lincoln, Massachusetts (1938), is a masterpiece of the new style. Mies van der Rohe's Farnsworth House in Plano, Illinois (1945–50), was a near-perfect example of a house as a pure volume of space enclosed by glass. Stunning in its beauty and simplicity, this stark home exemplified the ideals of a purist and ascetic Modernism.

Gropius and Mies had both been associated with the most famous design school in Europe, the Bauhaus in Germany. Gropius created it in 1919 in Weimar and designed its new headquarters in Dessau in 1926. The new Bauhaus provided houses for the master teachers that were demonstrations of the new esthetic. Mies directed the school between 1930 and 1933. The Bauhaus had replaced an earlier school of Arts and Crafts, and although the new school embraced mechanical production, it also advocated collaboration between the fine arts and design arts. The Bauhaus became synonymous with International style design, and its use of flat roofs and glass walls became its trademark.

The classroom building at the Bauhaus showcased a paradigmatic curtain wall of glass. It expressed a utopian program for the future, based on a quasi-mystical belief in the healthfulness and moral superiority of glass. The transparency and infinite variety of viewpoints were thought to dissolve the restrictions and barriers of the old order. Richard Neutra's Health House (1927–29), built in Los Angeles for Dr. Philip Lovell, embodied the belief that glass and sunlight led to improved health. Ironically, the glass architecture of the International style, which grew from utopian hopes of a transformed society, eventually became the favorite style of modern corporate architecture.

Surpassing even the architects of the International style with his experimental modernism, R. Buckminster Fuller created a visionary design called the Dymaxion House (1927–29). A hexagonal-plan house, suspended from a central mast, it was far ahead of its time and was too expensive to be built during the Depression. Some of the key ideas were reused in Fuller's Dymaxion Deployment Units, "dwelling machines" designed to address the great housing shortage at the end of the war. Some examples were built during the war using circular core units from silo factories. In 1945, an aluminum prototype was produced by Beech Aircraft of Wichita, Kansas, but it never went into mass production.

A number of other innovative architects demonstrated experimental homes at the Century of Progress Exposition in Chicago in 1933. George Fred Keck exhibited an all-glass house. Later, he and his brother William developed a successful practice in the Midwest, where they designed the first modern solar houses.

ART MODERNE —
1920-40

This style combined the sleek modernity of the International style with Art Deco ornament. Popularized by a Parisian exhibition in 1925, the Art Deco motif was used with great imagination and effect in skyscrapers, like the Chrysler Building. Art Moderne houses kept the flat roof of the International style, but added Art Deco's streamlined geometric forms and stylized details.

Above: Art Moderne house (c. 1930s), Miami Beach, Florida. These streamlined homes combined sophisticated Art Deco detailing and spare Modernist forms.

MODERN AGE—WORLD WAR II TO PRESENT

Ever since the Modernist movement discarded historical details, American architecture has been caught in a conflict between modern and traditional styles. Despite critical acclaim for spare Modernist buildings in the 1930s and 1940s, many Americans continued to prefer the styles rooted in European history. By the 1950s, the clean lines of Modernism had caught up with popular taste and many homeowners bought modern houses or began to strip away the historical features of older homes. But the tide turned again in the 1960s when a new generation began to restore old houses or add historical details to new ones. The 1960s was also the time when architects began to rebel against the purist ideology of Modernism by reintroducing historical details—albeit in completely new forms—to the world of high design. All of these forces led to a tremendous variety of styles in the modern age, few of which can be called truly modern or traditional.

RANCH AND SPLIT-LEVEL HOMES—1945-75

America's postwar population explosion produced a culture focused on family and middle-class domestic life. As thousands of soldiers returned from the war and started new families, suburban track housing became a new way of life. Modern and traditional styles merged in the postwar housing boom, producing new American prototypes that would become as well known as the log cabin. Ranch and split-level homes became a fixture of the American landscape, multiplying in planned communities such as Levittown on Long Island, New York. Although the development is frequently characterized as a symbol of featureless uniformity, it clearly served a need for quickly constructed, affordable homes after the war, and was replicated many times. In later years, many of the houses were expanded or altered to make them more individualized.

For the first time in a generation, new commercial buildings went up in major American cities. In Chicago, for example, no skyscraper had been built since the crash of 1929 and the resulting Depression. World War II had halted new construction projects as building materials went into the war

Above: Ranch house (c. 1950s), Waltham, Massachusetts. Ranch houses borrowed the low-pitched roof and horizontal windows of Prairie-school homes and California ranches. These features were greatly simplified within a basic formula for mass production.

effort. After the war, the International style innovation of glass and steel construction led to buildings that would become the first landmarks of high-rise America: the United Nations, Lever House (1952), and the Seagram Building in New York City. Mies van der Rohe also pioneered the development of skyscraper apartments in his 860–880 Lake Shore Drive towers in Chicago (1948–50).

Right: Ludwig Mies van der Rohe, Lake Shore Drive (1949), Chicago. Deceptively simple, these unembellished glass and steel towers are the visualization of Mies's dictum, "Less is more"—the mantra of the International style. They were the first high-rise apartment towers in the world.

CONTEMPORARY — 1940-1980s

The custom-designed homes and churches of this period often recast Modernist principles in unique forms. Richard Meier used the concrete and glass of the International style in an innovative cylinder and rectangular form for the Grotta House (984–89) that perfectly fits its hilly New Jersey site. The overall effect is more inviting than that of most International style homes, and also offers a convenient split-level layout. Eero Saarinen deliberately avoided the box shape in the Kresge Memorial Chapel (1954) at the Massachusetts Institute of Technology. This interdenominational chapel is a fifty-foot-wide brick cylinder set in a reflecting moat, evoking both modern and medieval forms.

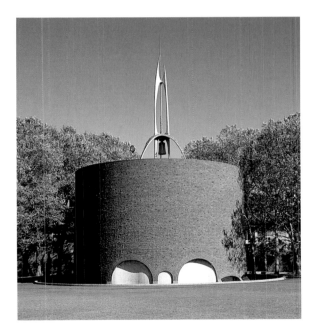

Left: Eero Saarinen, Kresge Memorial Chapel (1954). MIT, Cambridge, Massachusetts. This Modernist alternative to the boxy International style channels light into the building through a skylight and bands of windows at the base. The moat surrounding the building reflects light through the lower windows and creates a rippling effect inside the church.

Above: Richard Meier, Grotta House (1984–89), Harding Township, New Jersey. This house recasts the concrete and glass of the International style into an innovative form with a split-level floor plan.

Far right: Robert Venturi, Vanna Venturi House (1963), Chestnut Hill, Pennsylvania. This small house introduced the Postmodernist style with simplified versions or "historical quotations" of Classical details, including the broken pediment and mock arch above the front door.

POSTMODERNISM—1963 TO PRESENT

A few decades after Modernists rejected architectural history a new generation of Postmodernist architects revived it with a series of pointed references to the past. In response to Mies van der Rohe's
dictum, "Less is more," Robert Venturi argued, "Less is a bore." Venturi's first Postmodernist house incorporates understated Classical details in a modern form. Historical details became more pronounced in
the work of later Postmodernists, reaching a peak of exaggeration in the corporate towers designed
by Philip Johnson and John Burgee in the 1980s. Johnson, once a leading proponent of the International
style, injected wit, humor, and irony into these designs by adding large-scale historical features to modern skyscrapers. The best known is the Sony Building (1984) in New York City, a thirty-seven-story
tower topped by a gigantic Classical pediment.

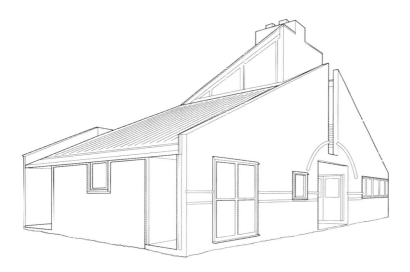

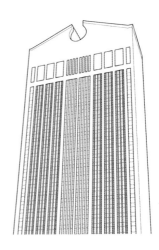

Right: Philip Johnson and John Burgee, Sony Building (1984), New York. The gigantic Classical pediment crowning the roof of this modern tower is a playful Postmodernist reference to the architectural past.

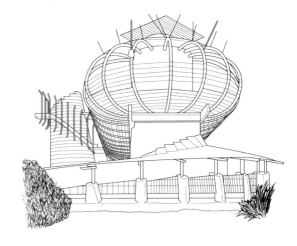

Right: Bart Prince, Bart Prince House (1984), Albuquerque, New Mexico. While the flowing style and materials recall Frank Lloyd Wright's organic architecture, the highly original forms defy categorization.

HISTORIC PRESERVATION

Historical styles came a long way in the twentieth century, developing from a Modernist anathema to a national cause. Americans once had a carefree disregard for old buildings, but after seeing so many destroyed in the path of rapid growth, the country became keenly aware of its lost heritage and made historic preservation a nationwide movement.

During the nineteenth century, despite the plethora of historic revivals, many old houses were torn down, even those belonging to such historic figures as John Hancock, whose house in Boston was demolished in 1863. Even Jefferson's Monticello was threatened. Paul Revere's house, saved in 1909, required extensive rebuilding. Used for commercial purposes, it had been drastically altered with an additional floor, eliminating the steep pitched roof. With a strong sense that the nation's history resides in its architecture, preservationists saved the Revere house and many other significant buildings.

In addition to individual houses, entire communities were rebuilt or restored, not always with archeological accuracy, as in Colonial Williamsburg, Virginia, begun in 1926. The William Penn House, known as Pennsbury Manor, was originally built between 1683 and 1699 in Morrisville, Pennsylvania. It was destroyed at the end of the eighteenth century, but re-created between 1933 and 1942. In keeping with the prevailing attitudes of the times, the focus in these restorations was on the homes of the wealthier classes. Only recently have pre–Civil War slave quarters and the homes of working-class residents of nineteenth-century industrial areas been deemed worthy of historic preservation. Today, many old mills and churches have also been adapted to new uses such as office, retail and apartment complexes. As the focus of preservation expands, even the artifacts of the early Modern period are now considered historic monuments; the 1938 house of architect Walter Gropius is now protected by the Society for the Preservation of New England Antiquities

LATE MODERN—1980s TO PRESENT

Today, historic features are at a peak of popularity—even in new construction. Many homes and suburban developments are being built with the roofs, windows, and door designs of eighteenth- and nineteenth-century styles, often on a much larger scale and in combinations that would never have

Right and far right: Thompson Vaivoda and Associates, Marilyn Moyer Meditation Chapel (1991), Portland, Oregon. The chapel is perched on the edge of a high cliff overlooking Portland. The large glass curtain wall extends over the cliff, creating an unobstructed connection to the dramatic view.

existed together in history. The Levittowns of today are highly nostalgic re-creations of the past. Yet from Times Square to Portland, Oregon, architects have also used the latest materials and technologies to create highly innovative buildings. Many are small in scale, but extraordinary in design. The New 42nd Street Studios (2000) on Times Square has made computerized lighting an integral and dynamic part of the design. Wrapped in glass and a high-tech grid of stainless steel louvers, the building is washed in changing colored lights that play off the façade. The Marilyn Moyer Meditation Chapel in Portland (1991) has a convex glass window perched on a high cliff, dissolving the barrier between viewer and nature. New York City's new planetarium, the Rose Center for Earth and Space (2000), is the latest addition to the nineteenth-century American Museum of Natural History, but its form—a six-story-high glass cube—is a radical departure from the museum's Beaux Arts style. Unique to their time, these buildings, and many others being built today, are part of the ever-changing history of American design.

Right: Platt, Byard, Dovell, New 42nd Street Studios (2000), New York. Lighting technology is an integral part of this design. Computerized colored lights play off the high-tech grid, creating a sophisticated version of a Times Square marquee. Called a "factory for the arts," the building provides studio space for nonprofit dance and theater groups.

Far right: Polshek Partnership, Rose Center for Earth and Space (2000), New York. The new plane-tarium is a six-story-high cube comprised of more than 700 panes of perfectly transparent glass. Nearly invisible stainless steel rods hold the panes, making them look like a single sheet of glass.

CHAPTER II
WINDOWS

Bringing light into buildings is an architectural art form—and the architect's medium is the window. Every detail of window design, from the size and shape of the pane to the clarity and color of the glass, affects the atmosphere inside a building and the connection to the outside world. From tiny leaded panes to glass walls, windows have framed our changing views.

Right: Church of St. Luke (1924), St. Paul, Minnesota. Rose window tracery.

Far right: Skidmore, Owings, and Merrill, Lever House (1952), New York. Glass curtain wall.

Glassmaking was an ancient art practiced by the Egyptians as early as 3500 BC. It was the Romans who developed clear glass and began to use it—sparingly—in the windows of important buildings. German craftsmen developed techniques for producing larger panes of glass in the eleventh century, but glazed windows were a great luxury, reserved for palaces and churches, up to the late Middle Ages.

European settlers brought the first glass windows to America. The northern Native American dwellings, which emphasized nomadic traditions and shelter from the elements, had precluded openings except for doors. The pueblos and adobe homes of the Southwest had small openings in stone to allow air circulation while keeping the heat out. The timber-framed homes of the early colonists replicated the windows of medieval times with small, thick panes of glass held together by lead strips. The Paul Revere House (1676) in Boston and many other early homes were built with these diamond-paned windows. The earliest type was a casement window that opened from side hinges.

Right: Paul Revere House (1676), Boston. Diamond-paned casement windows are medieval European features carried over to colonial American buildings.

Above: Stanley-Whitman House (c. 1720), Farmington, Connecticut. By the eighteenth century, New England saltbox homes, like this one, had sash windows with diamond panes.

Today's sash or double-hung window is not a modern invention. The modern style with separate top and bottom sections owes its origins to an obscure British law of 1709 that regulated building construction in London. At the time, windows had always been placed flush to the outside walls, held in place with wooden pins. For purposes of public safety, the law required that windows be recessed four inches, sitting more deeply into the interior of the façade. This modification created a window well large enough to hold the counterweights needed to lift sash windows and keep them open without the wooden pegs. While it would take another twenty years for sash windows to become a prevalent feature in most homes, in the process the modern window was born.

But the forces of fashion were also at work in the eighteenth century and led to more elaborate designs. The three-part Palladian window, named for the Italian Classical architect Andrea Palladio, became a key feature of Georgian and Federalist buildings. Placed over the door and surrounded by sash windows and fanlights, the Palladian window was the centerpiece of Classical symmetry.

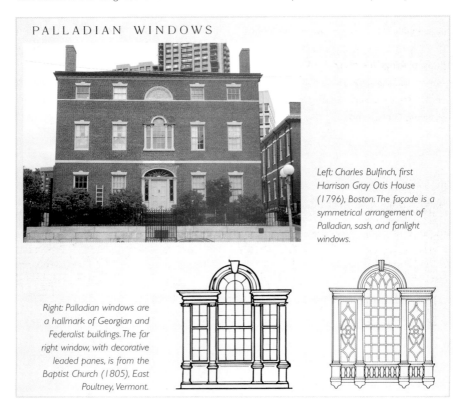

PALLADIAN WINDOWS

Left: Charles Bulfinch, first Harrison Gray Otis House (1796), Boston. The façade is a symmetrical arrangement of Palladian, sash, and fanlight windows.

Right: Palladian windows are a hallmark of Georgian and Federalist buildings. The far right window, with decorative leaded panes, is from the Baptist Church (1805), East Poultney, Vermont.

At first, American churches used the same window styles as those in colonial homes. But no style would have as great an impact on church design, particularly on windows, as Gothic Revival. Ever since the Middle Ages, lancet windows with tall, pointed arches had been used to stream light into churches and cathedrals, symbolizing the presence of God. Intersecting arches and stained glass transformed light into a multitude of colors and patterns. Circular rose windows added complexity with patterned tracery—wheel spokes, quatrefoils, and flowing and undulating curves. Gothic Revival churches used the same forms, with such great effect that the style spread to synagogues, homes, and public buildings. The residents of nineteenth-century New England cottages and southern plantations alike looked out through lancet windows with stained glass and intricate tracery. Even early skyscrapers, like the Woolworth Building in New York City (1913), "the Cathedral of Commerce," soared with elaborate Gothic windows on each of its sixty stories.

Above (from left to right): Sash, oval, and fanlight windows from the Federalist period.

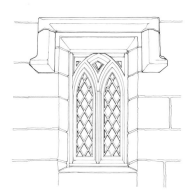

Above: Lancet and quatrefoil windows from Gothic Revival churches.

Above and right: Schneider and Herter, Park East Synagogue (1890), New York. The large rose window is in the Romanesque style. The drawing shows details of the smaller multifoil windows, derived from the Great Mosque in Crdoba, Spain.

Left: Rose Hill Plantation House
(1858), Bluffton, South Carolina.
Gothic Revival lancet windows.

Below: Cass Gilbert, Woolworth
Building (1913), New York. Neo
Gothic windows.

Right: Daniel Burnham and John Wellborn Root, Reliance Building (1895), Chicago. The building pioneered the use of large windows and slender metal framing. It is the first example of the "Chicago window," a wide fixed pane flanked by narrow movable sash windows.

At the same time that American architecture took on a spiritual quality, it was transformed by the Industrial Revolution. The single most dramatic change in building design—the evolution of the steel and glass skyscraper—was achieved with three industrial innovations in the late nineteenth century: steel building frames, high-speed elevators, and new methods for manufacturing plate glass. Chicago's Reliance Building (1895) led the way to the new era. A steel skeleton liberated the fourteen-story building from the weighty stone walls of the past. Large sheets of glass, strong enough to withstand the elements, were framed between the slender steel piers, opening the building to unlimited daylight and a new lightness in design.

But not everyone followed the new window trend. Another early steel frame building in Chicago, the Newberry Library (1892), artfully displays the long, narrow windows of the Romanesque style. In the 1880s, Henry Hobson Richardson used eyebrow dormers that barely broke the skin of his Shingle-style roofs. In 1911, Gustav Stickley, a leader of the Craftsman movement, designed log cabins with diamond-paned windows, a deliberate throwback to medieval window styles. Prairie-school architects also reintroduced leaded glass windows, but often used machine-cut glass in geometric designs.

Left Henry Ives Cobb, Newberry Library (1892), Chicago. Romanesque Revival windows.

*Right: Henry Hobson Richardson,
heavy-lidded dormer windows
barely break through the roof of
the Shingle-style Ames Gate Lodge
(1881), North Easton,
Massachusetts.*

*Below: Gustav Stickley
reintroduced medieval diamond-
paned windows in the cabins
of Craftsman Farms (1911),
Parsippany, New York.*

Above: William Gray Purcell and George Grant Elmslie, Purcell-Cutts House (1913), Minneapolis, Minnesota.
Prairie-style homes used a running series of detailed windows

But plate-glass windows were here to stay. With manufacturing improvements, large windows were hung like a curtain on steel frames and became entire walls of glass in office and apartment towers. The United Nations Secretariat Building (1949) was New York City's first glass curtain wall building and was followed by glass towers throughout the country. Churches also adopted the technique. In 1947, Frank Lloyd Wright used a glass curtain wall to project dramatically out of a masonry church. By 1980, some churches, like Philip Johnson's "Crystal Cathedral," were all glass and steel.

Above: Roche Dinkeloo Associates. This sweeping view of the Manhattan skyline illustrates the evolution of architectural glass, from the city's first glass curtain wall in the United Nations Secretariat Building (1949), left, to the taut folds of glass enveloping the United Nations Plaza buildings (1976–83), right.

Right: Lohan Caprile Goettsch, UBS Tower (2001), Chicago. The city's first office tower of the twenty-first century elevates glass and steel construction to a new level of high-tech design. The principal partner in the architecture firm, Dirk Lohan, is the grandson of Mies van der Rohe.

Right: Frank Lloyd Wright, Unitarian Meeting House (1947), Madison, Wisconsin. The projecting window was a striking departure from the flat or recessed windows of earlier churches.

Left: Philip Johnson and John
Burgee, Garden Grove Church, the
"Crystal Cathedral" (1980), Los
Angeles. The glass and steel
building is both a church and
a studio set for a televangelist.

Modernist architects used skyscraper techniques on a domestic scale, sheathing houses in slender steel and glass grids. Ludwig Mies van der Rohe and Philip Johnson took the concept even further by eliminating the grid and creating virtually all-glass houses. Windows became the single, transparent boundary around the home's interior space. Striking in their beauty and simplicity, glass houses, however, were not for everyone. Homeowners with a more guarded sense of privacy much preferred the 1950s-era style of suburban America—the picture window. Today, many are more concerned with a window's environmental advantages and have switched to skylights and solar energy panels—often incorporated within historical-style homes.

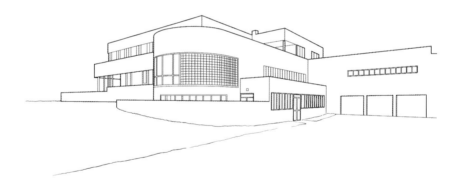

Above: Edward Durrell Stone, Mandel House (1934), Bedford Hills, New York. Ribbon windows and glass brick corners are distinctive features of International-style houses.

Below: Ludwig Mies van der Rohe, Farnsworth House (1945–51), Plano, Illinois. This landmark of the International style demonstrated the Modernist concept of buildings as transparent enclosures of space.

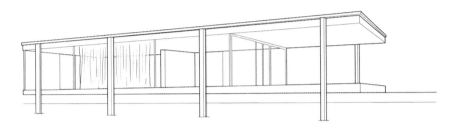

Left: Neo-Stick-style house, Stony Creek, Connecticut. Windows with environmental advantages are common in today's homes. Solar energy panels are enclosed here in a Stick-style wooden dome. Skylights have replaced the more traditional dormers in the pitched roof.

Whether they swing, slide, or slam, doors satisfy a wide sweep of human needs. They hold the key to privacy and security, and can be inviting or intimidating, awesome or foreboding. Changing door designs also say a great deal about the life and times of the people behind the door.

Right: Door of St. Elizabeth's Chapel (1914), Sudbury, Massachusetts. The elaborate ironwork on this door was designed by the period's most ardent proponent of authentic Gothic architecture, Ralph Adams Cram. His Neo-Gothic masterpiece is the Cathedral of St. John the Divine in New York City.

Above: McPhedris-Warner House (1718–23), Portsmouth, New Hampshire. The door is framed by a Georgian rounded pediment and Corinthian pilasters.

Above: Wentworth-Gardner House (1760), Portsmouth, New Hampshire. A Georgian swan's neck pediment crowns the doorway.

Above: A swan's neck pediment and elaborately carved columns adorn the Georgian doorway of this Massachusetts house.

In America's early, precarious days of colonial settlement, doors were built with more attention to strength than beauty. Heavy timbers, joined by crossed planks, were held in place with iron hinges and latches. Doors had little, if any, embellishment; the handcrafted ironwork was the only ornamentation, and windows in doors were rare. Style did not become a significant consideration until the more civilized times of the eighteenth century when Georgian architecture opened the door to an expansive menu of Classical details. For architects of the period the main entryway was the key feature of the façade. Doors were set in the center and framed with Greek and Roman columns and pediments. Columns of every Classical order and pediments of varying shape—triangular, rounded, segmental, or open at the top—were formally arranged to complement the symmetry of the exterior design. Fanlights above and sidelights on either side of the door filled entrance halls with light while maintaining privacy and security.

Above: Charles Bulfinch, first Harrison Gray Otis House (1796), Boston. A Federalist doorway with a fanlight and sidelights.

Early colonial churches were plain meetinghouses, yet they often framed their entrance doors with Classical details.

Above: St. Paul's Church (1707), Wickford, Rhode Island. This simple meetinghouse has a Georgian swan's neck pediment and pilasters framing its doors.

Doorways were not only the first sign of a church's style, but also offered a clue to the congregation's frame of mind. In the early nineteenth century, the Gothic and Greek Revival styles competed head to head, and each style was seen as a different approach to life. In contrast to Greek Revival's symmetry, Gothic architecture's irregular forms were considered progressive. Religious groups often chose one style or the other as a badge of identity. A battle ensued in the First Congregational Society of Uxbridge, Massachusetts soon after the congregation built a Greek Revival church in 1833. The following year, a split between Unitarian and Calvinist factions led the Unitarians to build a Gothic Revival church directly across the street. The distinctive doorways are clear signs of the different camps. A conservative Classical portico encloses the square doors of the Greek Revival church. A soaring tower and Gothic window rise up from the arched door of the Gothic Revival. But in many cases, the two styles peacefully coincided with porticos, pediments, and pointed arches in a single church.

Above: First Evangelical Congregational Church (1833), Uxbridge, Massachusetts. Greek Revival doorway with a Classical portico.

Above: First Congregational Society (1834), Unitarian, Uxbridge, Massachusetts. A split in the congregation between Calvinists and Unitarians led the Unitarians to build this Gothic Revival Church across the street from the original Greek Revival building.

Above: St. John's Episcopal Church (1831), East Poultney, Vermont. A combination of a Greek Revival pediment and Gothic pointed arches.

Triple-door entrances in Christian churches are imbued with religious significance as symbols of the Holy Trinity. The tradition carried over from such great European cathedrals as Notre Dame to French Gothic revivals such as the Cathedral of St. John the Divine in New York City. In 1961, Modernist architect Marcel Breuer designed a strikingly original version in wood, concrete, and steel in St. John's Abbey in Collegeville, Minnesota (1961). New York City's new planetarium, the Rose Center for Earth and Space (2000), is called the "Cosmic Cathedral" by its architect, James Polshek. The entrance to this transparent building is an all-glass, triple doorway of revolving doors.

Above: Ralph Adams Cram, Cathedral of St. John the Divine (begun in 1893), New York. French Gothic doorway.

Left: St. John's Abbey, door
detail. Three wooden doors are
enclosed by a boxy concrete
portico and dramatically set within
the arched base of the enormous
bell tower.

Left: Marcel Breuer, St. John's
Abbey (1961), Collegeville,
Minnesota. Designed by a founder
of the International style, this
church is nevertheless a radical
departure. Breuer's design creates
a powerful sense of spirituality far
removed from the machinelike
functionalism of early Modernism.

Far left: Polshek Partnership, doorway of the Rose Center for Earth
and Space (2000), the Hayden
Planetarium, New York.

One of the most distinctive doorway features in American architecture is the Richardsonian arch, named for its designer, Henry Hobson Richardson. The massive form that bears his name is a powerful arch that he used as a dominant feature in churches, public buildings, and homes. Broad, rounded, and composed of large, rugged stones, the Richardsonian arch was embraced by such renowned architects as Louis Sullivan and Dankmar Adler. Their inspired version is the great semicircular arch framing the doorway of the Pilgrim Baptist Church in Chicago (1891), originally built as a synagogue. They used it again in the triple-arched stone doorway of Chicago's Auditorium Building (1886–96). More than half a century later, Frank Lloyd Wright, who had worked for Sullivan during the construction of the auditorium, designed his own Richardsonian-inspired arch, the broad yet intricate brick span over the Morris Gift Shop in San Francisco.

Right: Henry Hobson Richardson, Ames Gate Lodge (1881), North Easton, Massachusetts. Richardsonian arch.

Far right: Louis Sullivan and Dankmar Adler, Pilgrim Baptist Church (originally built as a synagogue, 1891), Chicago. Arched entrance.

פתחו לי שערי צדק אבא בם כם אודה יה

OPEN FOR ME THE GATES OF RIGHTEOUSNESS,
THAT I MAY ENTER THROUGH THEM, TO PRAISE THE LORD.

Above: Frank Lloyd Wright, Morris Gift Shop (1948), San Francisco.

Left: Louis Sullivan and Dankmar Adler, Auditorium Building (1886–90), Chicago. The massive arched doorways provide a dramatic entrance to the theater.

Wright and other Prairie-school architects designed new cubic-shaped doorways that are devoid of Classical details. Yet these designers share a common approach with Georgian architects in making the door a key feature of the house, a practice that would change in the modern age. While Art Moderne houses of the 1920s and 1930s introduced glass brick fanlights and sidelights, doors virtually disappeared in the minimalist homes of the 1940s and 1950s. Sliding glass doors were introduced in this period and others were often understated or hidden from view. The transparent portals of corporate towers often focus on the impressive lobbies inside.

Left: Richard E. Schmidt and Hugh M. G. Garden, Madlener House (1902), Chicago. An exquisite doorway in a Prairie-style house

Below (left, detail, and right): Frank Lloyd Wright, Winslow House (1894), River Forest, Illinois. The front door of this early Prairie house displays Classical symmetry in a new cubic form. This house was Wright's first independent commission after leaving Louis Sullivan's firm.

Right: Lohan Caprile Goettsch, UBS (Union Bank of Switzerland) Tower (2001), Chicago. Ultratransparent glass panels provide an impressive view of the spacious lobby.

Door design suffered its greatest slight in the mid-twentieth century when suburban homes made garage doors more prominent than entrances for people. Screen doors added insult to injury, completely covering any detail in the main door—like a hairnet over a coiffure. But the trend seems to be changing as homeowners seek out doors with historic features. Today, every local home supply store offers front doors with leaded window designs.

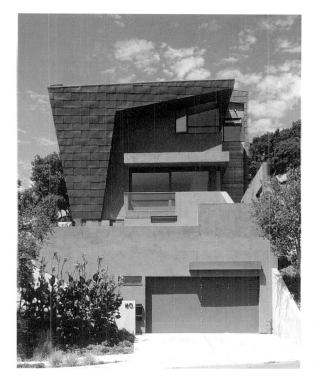

Left: Franklin D. Israel, Drager House (1995), Oakland, California. The prominence of the garage door, even in high-design houses like this one, acknowledges the overriding importance of the automobile.

CHAPTER IV
ROOFS

High or low, pitched or flat, shingled or tiled, a roof is the first requirement for shelter. Yet even in earliest times, roofs were shaped by esthetic and cultural values. Like their Native American predecessors, European settlers covered their homes and houses of worship with materials readily at hand. But the forms they built were part of the long tradition of following familiar styles.

Right: Kiva, Escalante Pueblo (c. AD 900–1300), New Mexico. Native Americans of the Southwest built kivas or ceremonial rooms within their pueblos. Excavated deep within the ground, the kiva was roofed over with poles representing aspects of the creation myth. The shafts of sunlight that fell through the poles created a mysterious effect within the excavation and provided geothermal heat for the cold desert nights.

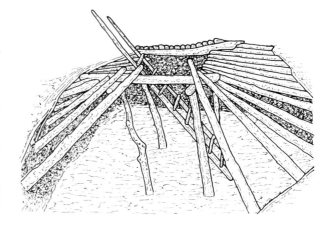

The typical shape of colonial American roofs was taken from the pitched roof of medieval Europe. Pitched roofs were built to shed rain and snow, but the shape of the roof end, known as a gable, was a sign of cultural style. The most distinctive was the stepped gable, characteristic of Dutch and Flemish settlements. English, Dutch, and Swedish settlers also used gambrel roofs which have two angles of pitch and are curved or sloped at the sides. Each group of colonists had its own gable and gambrel variations, many of which continue in home building today. Gambrels were more difficult to build than simple triangular gables but provided more space in the upper floors. In the arid Southwest, Spanish colonists built flat roofs of tile or adobe to ward off sun and heat. Adobe, sun-baked mud, was an American and Spanish tradition. Native Americans used it to build pueblos centuries before the Spanish arrived, and the Moors introduced it in Spain.

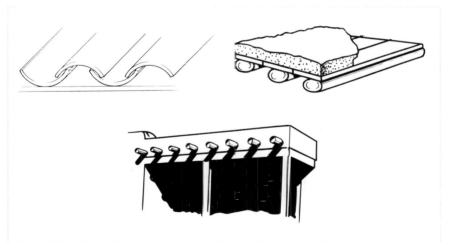

Above: Originally found in Florida and the Southwest, Spanish or Mission-style roof tiles have spread to homes throughout the United States. Roofs made of adobe with exposed vigas or beams are native to both Spain and the Southwest. They became popular again in the Pueblo Revival style of the 1920s

Above: Old Ship Meeting House (1681), Hingham, Massachusetts. Originally built with a gambrel roof, this meetinghouse, the oldest of its kind in New England, was expanded in the eighteenth century with a hipped roof topped by a balustrade, cupola, and steeple.

Hipped roofs, which slope upward from all four sides of a building, created a lower and more sophisticated profile than a gable, and were popular in Georgian buildings of the eighteenth century. The Italianate style of the mid-nineteenth century introduced flat rooflines decorated with heavy cornices and large, elaborate brackets. But the great variety of European Revival styles flooding the country in the nineteenth century made it hard to identify cultural origins or architectural periods. Roofs that were once defining features were mixed with a host of popular details. Cornices and brackets, for example, became the prevailing style and were added to many different kinds of roofs.

Above: Italianate roofs have overhanging eaves supported by elaborate brackets. Pattern books offered a range of bracket designs.

Left: Italianate villa, Haddam, Connecticut.

Above: Ruskinian Gothic house (c. 1880s), Newton, Massachusetts. The ornate gambrel roof has multicolored shingles and elaborate dormers in the High Gothic style promoted by the British art critic John Ruskin.

But there was no mistaking the Second Empire period, the style that defined an entire age with one type of roof, the mansard. Named for its inventor, the seventeenth-century French architect François Mansart, the style was revived in the Second Empire of Napoleon III (1852–70) when many parts of Paris were rebuilt with mansard roofs. The style became enormously popular in America at the same time. Resembling a top hat with curves, the mansard roof offered esthetic and practical advantages. Its high profile made it a frequent choice for new government buildings, including Washington, D.C.'s Old Executive Office Building, Philadelphia's City Hall, and the New York State Capitol at Albany.

Left: Thomas Fuller, Isaac Perry, Leopold Eidlitz, and Henry Hobson Richardson, New York State Capitol (1867–99), Albany. The Second Empire style was at the peak of its popularity when construction of the capitol began in 1867. Finally completed thirty-two years later by a succession of architects, the building was a bit out of style, but the high profile of the mansard roof still made a splendid impression.

Homeowners also appreciated the roomy insides, a full story of usable attic space. American cities and small towns lined their streets with mansard buildings, taking pride in their French sophistication. However, the style was expensive and it ended in America with the financial panic of 1873, shortly after Napoleon III's downfall.

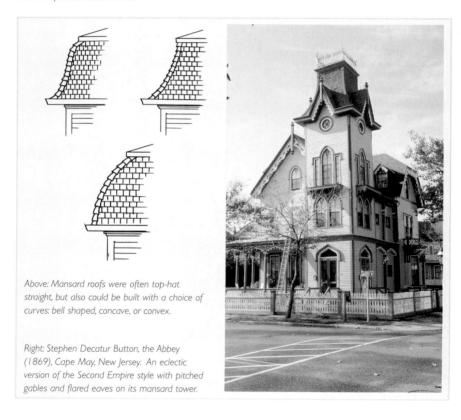

Above: Mansard roofs were often top-hat straight, but also could be built with a choice of curves: bell shaped, concave, or convex.

Right: Stephen Decatur Button, the Abbey (1869), Cape May, New Jersey. An eclectic version of the Second Empire style with pitched gables and flared eaves on its mansard tower.

Wealthy Americans continued to build extravagant homes throughout the century, adjusting their rooflines to new fashions. The Châteauesque roof, sharply pitched or hipped with elaborate dormers, was popular in both summer estates and city mansions. In the resort communities of Newport, Cape Cod, and Maine, many large summer houses were built in the Shingle style. One building could incorporate several different roofs—gabled, hipped, and conical—all covered with a continuous skin of overlapping shingles. However complex the roofline, the overall effect was a unified, smooth expanse.

Above: Richard Morris Hunt, Ogden Goelet House (1892) Salve Regina University, Newport, Rhode Island. French châteaux were the inspiration for these sharply pitched and hipped roofs.

Right: St. Paul's Episcopal Church (1883), Newtown Highlands, Massachusetts. Shingle-style roofs were most common in homes, but also wrapped themselves around churches, including the steeples.

Shingle-style roofs came within reach of average Americans across the country with the introduction of the Craftsman bungalow in the early twentieth century. For the first time in popular American architecture, the historical precedent came not from Europe, but from Asia. The predominant features of these low, shingled roofs were overhanging eaves and rafters, influenced by Japanese buildings.

Right: Bell Bungalow (1920s), Cape May, New Jersey. Craftsman bungalows with low roofs and overhanging eaves became one of America's most popular housing styles for middle-class families. The style was introduced in California and spread through the country with kits of precut lumber, fixtures, and fittings.

Above: Otis Townsend House, (1915) Cape May, New Jersey. This rare three-story bungalow is capped by an unusual roof called a jerkin-head, named for its resemblance to a type of jacket or vest.

With new materials and technologies, modern roofs became more than just roofs. They also took on the role of walls, windows, steeples, and sculpture. International-style architect Rudolf Schindler invented the A-frame house in 1934 by bringing the steep pitch of Tudor style roofs down to the ground in one monumental gable.

Above: A-frame house (c. 1980), Woodstock, Vermont. This popular vacation home model was invented in 1934 by International-style architect Rudolf Schindler, who based it on Tudor Revival houses.

Left: Tudor Revival cottage (c. 1920s), Mendon, Vermont. The steeply pitched roof was derived from English medieval architecture. The style was widely spread in the 1920s and 1930s by mail-order catalogs that offered plans and kits for several Tudor models.

The roof is also the predominant feature of Frank Lloyd Wright's Beth Sholom Synagogue in suburban Philadelphia and of the Eduardo Catalano House in North Carolina. The swooping roof of Trinity Church in Rocky Point, New York, takes the shape of a fish, a Christian symbol, with the fish tail serving as the church steeple. The soaring roof of the Air Force Academy Chapel in Colorado Springs is an abstract construction of glass tetrahedrons that serves as roof, windows, tower, and steeple.

Above: Frank Lloyd Wright, Beth Sholom Synagogue (1954–59), Elkins Park, Pennsylvania. The tent-like roof was designed as a symbol of Mount Sinai where Moses received the Ten Commandments. This "mountain of light" holds translucent plastic panes that filter light into the sanctuary by day and glow from within at night.

Right: Eduardo Catalano, Catalano House (built in 1955, demolished in 2001), Raleigh, North Carolina. The roof was the primary element of the house.

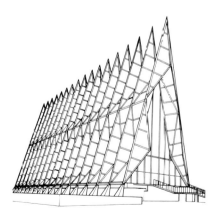

Above: Edward Slater, Trinity Church (1964), Rocky Point, New York. Known as the "Fish Church," this unusual building was one of the Expressionist forms created by Modernist architects in reaction to the stark designs of the International style.

Left: Skidmore, Owings, and Merrill, Air Force Academy Chapel, (1956–62), Colorado Springs, Colorado. The abstract construction of tetrahedrons serves as roof, walls, windows, and steeple.

Postmodernists have achieved dramatic results with shed roofs, from beach houses to Frank Gehry's sculptural counterpoints in stainless steel. The sharply sloped roof of the Citicorp Center (1977) in New York was originally designed to hold solar panels. However, the high price of the equipment would have surpassed the potential savings in energy costs. Nonetheless, the roof has become a distinctive profile on the New York City skyline.

Right: Beach house (c. 1980), West Hampton, Long Island, New York. Shed roofs in counterpointing directions are a feature of the Postmodernist style.

Left: Hugh Stubbins and
Associates, Citicorp Center (1977),
New York. The sharply angled roof
has become the building's icon.

CHAPTER V
DOMES

Domes are uncommon roofs, built throughout history to create a true sense of the extraordinary. And they require extraordinary engineering. The great domes of the world are milestones of innovative and Herculean construction—from the Pantheon in Rome (AD 120) to the Duomo in Florence (1420–36) and St. Paul's Cathedral in London (1696–1708).

Soon after America achieved its independence, the new republic sought its own national monument, a great dome to top the Capitol in Washington, D.C.

Right: Thomas U. Walter, U.S. Capitol dome (1856–63), Washington, D.C. Although the Capitol dome was one of the first to use prefabricated cast iron, its height is based on the same device used in the Duomo in fifteenth-century Florence— building two domes in one. The large outer dome is held up by a ring of curved iron ribs. Underneath is a smaller, self-supporting dome, visible only from the inside.

The task would take not one but two domes. The first, completed in 1824, was made of wood sheathed in copper. But nearly everyone thought it looked like an ungainly helmet, and it was eventually removed in 1856. Work on the second dome was interrupted by the outbreak of the Civil War in 1861. President Abraham Lincoln kept the construction going until the dome was completed in 1863. Topped by the twenty-foot-high Statue of Freedom, it is a powerful symbol of the nation's solidarity.

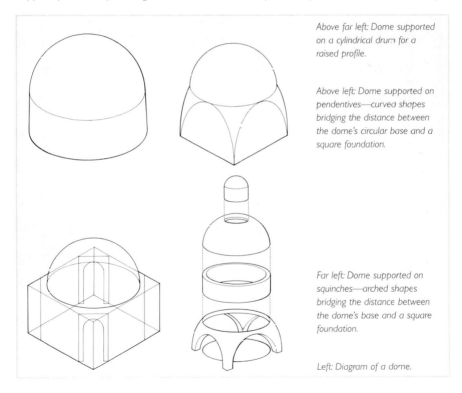

Above far left: Dome supported on a cylindrical drum for a raised profile.

Above left: Dome supported on pendentives—curved shapes bridging the distance between the dome's circular base and a square foundation.

Far left: Dome supported on squinches—arched shapes bridging the distance between the dome's base and a square foundation.

Left: Diagram of a dome.

The enormous weight and huge span of the world's great domes demanded innovative construction techniques. The Pantheon dome rests on a massive circular base, with walls almost twenty feet thick. The Byzantine architects who built Hagia Sophia, in Istanbul, Turkey, used a square base supported by curved triangular panels called pendentives. The Duomo, St. Peter's, and St. Paul's used huge chains to reinforce the base. These devices and many others contain the outward thrust of the domes' great height and mass. The United States Capitol, which most closely resembles St. Paul's, was one of the first prefabricated cast-iron domes and weighs nearly nine million pounds. In the twentieth century, Italian architect-engineer Pier Luigi Nervi revolutionized dome construction with new techniques in poured concrete that greatly reduced weight loads. The culmination of his work created a new domed landmark in Rome, a circular ribbed stadium built in 1960.

Nearly every state in the union has put a dome on its statehouse to achieve height and grandeur. One of the earliest was installed in 1797 in Boston. It was originally covered in gray-painted copper sheeting applied by Paul Revere and Sons in 1802. The striking twenty-three-karat gilding was not applied until 1874. One of the largest and most unusual domes on a government building appeared in the modern age: the Thompson Center, the Illinois State office building in Chicago, is a sixteen-story, 160-foot-diameter, glass and steel dome.

*Right: Charles Bulfinch,
Massachusetts State House
(1795–97), Boston. Originally
covered with copper made by Paul
Revere's company, the dome got
its twenty-three-karat gilding in
1874 and has glittered ever since
on top of Beacon Hill.*

Above: Helmut Jahn, James R. Thompson Center (1985), Chicago. The center is a transparent
rotunda, a 1.2-million-square-foot space under glass.

Although the word *dome* derives from the Latin *domicile*, the great effort and expense of building a dome made it a rare feature in domestic architecture. Thomas Jefferson's Virginia country estate, Monticello, is a beautiful exception.

Right: Thomas Jefferson, Monticello (1769–82/ 1796–1809), near Charlottesville, Virginia. Jefferson drew on two models for the dome: a Palladian villa from sixteenth-century Italy, and a Parisian town house built during his ambassadorship in France.

Widely read in Classical architecture, Jefferson closely followed the plans of Palladio's Villa Rotonda from the Italian Renaissance. But he also was strongly influenced by the contemporary architecture that he saw in Paris during his term as Minister to France. One especially impressive town house was the model for the dome in Monticello. The spacious rotunda in another Jefferson landmark, the University of Virginia Library, inspired the use of domes in many other American libraries.

Left: Philip Armour House (1860), Irvington-on-Hudson, New York. Domes or houses are almost as rare as octagon houses. This unusual combination is one of the few surviving octagon houses.

In the early twentieth century, Buckminster Fuller tried to bring the dome down to earth as an inexpensive, easily built house. His Dymaxion House of 1927 was a combination of modern technology and primitive forms. The prefabricated structure was built from the base of farm silos with a yurtlike roof copied from Mongolian huts. Fuller is better known for his later invention, the geodesic dome, a preformed metal or plastic frame covered with a plastic skin. Although he designed both models for mass production, neither was conventional or comfortable enough to satisfy popular taste. Another inexpensive domed innovation, the concrete balloon house, also remains an interesting oddity.

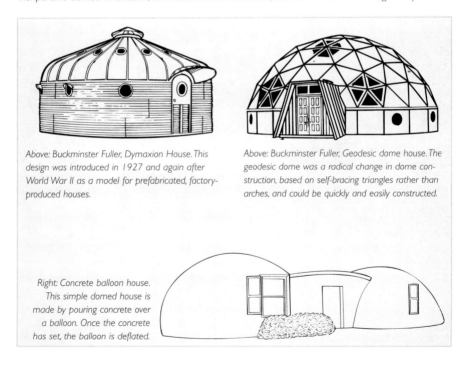

Above: Buckminster Fuller, Dymaxion House. This design was introduced in 1927 and again after World War II as a model for prefabricated, factory-produced houses.

Above: Buckminster Fuller, Geodesic dome house. The geodesic dome was a radical change in dome construction, based on self-bracing triangles rather than arches, and could be quickly and easily constructed.

Right: Concrete balloon house. This simple domed house is made by pouring concrete over a balloon. Once the concrete has set, the balloon is deflated.

However, the geodesic dome was a quick, cheap way to create a giant enclosure and became well known as an impressive symbol of futuristic design at world fairs in the 1960s. Fuller later made headlines when he proposed a geodesic dome over Manhattan, although the idea never got beyond a fantasy. The best-known geodesic structure in the world today is in Disney's Epcot Center in Orlando, Florida. Another American dome landmark is the Houston Astrodome (1965), the first ballpark with a roof enclosing its playing field. Since grass would not grow inside the park, it also led to the first artificial grass, Astroturf. Later models, like the Toronto Skydome, developed retractable roofs.

Above: Houston Astrodome (1965). Big enough to contain an eighteen-story building, the Astrodome was the first covered baseball park and became the model for indoor sports stadiums throughout the world. Newer models have retractable roofs.

As in civic buildings, the dome has achieved its unique potential in many of America's great houses of worship. The hemispherical shape of the dome has expressed spiritual qualities since ancient times, not only in churches, synagogues, and mosques, but also in such Native American structures as the Navajo's dome-shaped hogans of wood and earth, built to reflect the sacred dome of heaven.

Steeples and towers were more common than domes in seventeenth- and eighteenth-century American churches, but large domes were on the rise in the nineteenth century. The New Old South Church in Boston (1875) has a vibrant, eclectic dome, freely combined with Gothic towers and pinnacles. Another impressive dome rose in Boston atop the Mother Church of the Christian Science Center.

Right: Charles A. Cummings and Willard T. Sears, New Old South Church (1875), Boston. In vibrant High Gothic style, the pinnacled dome tops a colorful tower.

Far right: Charles Brigham and S. Beman, Mother Church, Christian Science Center (1906), Boston. This Beaux Arts addition to the original church features a large dome on a drum, similar to those on St. Peter's in Rome and St. Paul's Cathedral in London.

Brightly colored mosaic domes adorn Byzantine Revival churches, including two of the largest in the country, St. Bartholomew's in New York City (1919) and the National Shrine of the Immaculate Conception (1920) in Washington, D.C. Frank Lloyd Wright reinterpreted the Byzantine dome in a futuristic design for the Annunciation Greek Orthodox Church (1956) in Wauwatosa, Wisconsin. The low-lying domed building is part Byzantine church and part flying saucer.

Left: Maginnis and Wa.sh,
Frederick Vernon Murphy, National
Shrine of the Immaculate
Conception (1920), Washington,
D.C. The mosaic covered dome is
in the Byzantine Revival style.

Far left: Frank Lloyd Wright
Annunciation Greek Orthodox
Church (1956), Wauwatosa,
Wisconsin. The futuristic domed
church looks like a Byzantine
style flying saucer.

Above: Charles R. Greco, Temple Beth Israel (1936), West Hartford, Connecticut. The flattened ribbed dome reveals an Art Deco influence.

Wright used another low, broad dome in one of his last and most ambitious projects, the Marin County Civic Center (1959) outside of San Francisco. A golden tower rises like a minaret beside the dome, giving the center the air of a Modernist mosque. True mosques with traditional and unusual domes were built in the late twentieth century, including more than one hundred in New York City alone. Eastern religious groups also built striking domed houses of worship in America, such as the exotic Baha'i Temple (1920–53) and New England Peace Pagoda (1985).

Above: Frank Lloyd Wright, Marin County Civic Center (1959) Marin County, California. The shallow dome recalls the futuristic design of Wright's earlier Annunciation Greek Orthodox Church. The gold tower is a dramatic exclamation point.

Above: Skidmore, Owings, and Merrill, Islamic Cultural Center (1991), New York. The ribbed dome rises from a stepped, pyramidal base.

Right: Jean-Baptiste Louis Bourgeois, Baha'i Temple (1920–53), Wilmette, Illinois. The Baha'i faith originated in Iran, but the style of the temple, sometimes called "Chicago's Taj Mahal," is an eclectic mix of Eastern influences.

Far right: Nipponzan Myohoji Sangha, New England Peace Pagoda (1985), Leverett, Massachusetts. The dome is based on a sacred mountain shape from Buddhist architecture.

The Classical column came to the New World in the collective memory of European settlers. It became part of the universal language of architects from ancient Greece and Rome to Renaissance Italy, Georgian England, and Thomas Jefferson's America. A trickle of Classical features can be seen in the simple columns on the doorways of some seventeenth-century American homes and churches. The flood of fully detailed columns flowed in from eighteenth-century Georgian England and widened into a Greek Revival river of columned porticos in the first half of the nineteenth century.

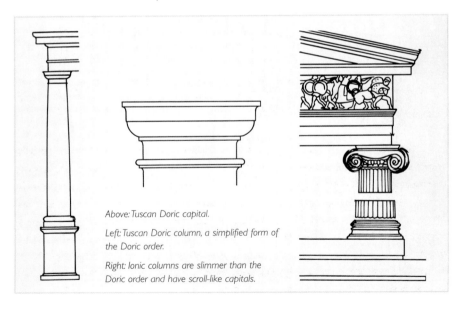

Above: Tuscan Doric capital.

Left: Tuscan Doric column, a simplified form of the Doric order.

Right: Ionic columns are slimmer than the Doric order and have scroll-like capitals.

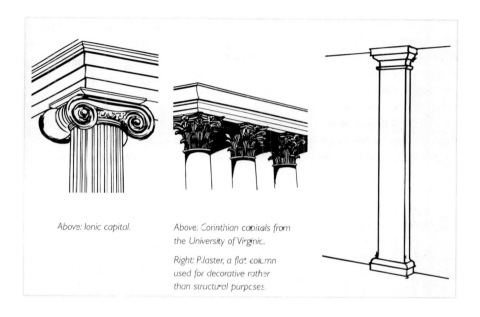

Above: Ionic capital.

Above: Corinthian capitals from the University of Virginia.

Right: Pilaster, a flat column used for decorative rather than structural purposes.

Greek Classicism is based on different forms of architectural expression, called orders, each with its own set of proportions and decorative motifs. The key to each order is the column, which defines the characteristics of the entire building. Doric columns are the simplest and heaviest; Ionic are more delicate, with slender, fluted shafts and twin scrolls at the top; Corinthian are the most slender and ornate, with elaborate bases and tall, decorative capitals resembling a basket filled with acanthus leaves. Variations include the Tuscan order, a simplified form of Doric, and the Composite, an embellished form incorporating elements from all the other column styles. Columns were originally designed to support the roofs of Greek and Roman buildings, but Georgian and Federalist styles often used pilasters, a flattened representation of a Classical column, as pure decoration.

In the Greek Revival era, columns of each type sprouted up on every kind of building across America, from New England homes and universities to southern plantations and California missions.

Left: Folk-style Greek Revival house (c. 1840), Wickford, Rhode Island. One of the simplest Greek Revival forms, this typical gable house has vertical boards at the corners that give the appearance of pilasters.

Far left: Lady Pepperell House (1760), Kittery Point, Maine. An elegant house with Georgian pilasters.

*Right: San Francisco de Asis
(1782–91), San Francisco. A
Spanish mission church with
heavy Doric columns.*

Left: Abner Cook, builder, Sweetbrush (1852), Austin, Texas. Double-height Ionic Columns.

Below: Ithiel Town and Andrew Jackson Davis, Russell House (1830), Wesleyan University, Middletown, Connecticut. Corinthian columns designed by two major American architects of the Greek Revival period.

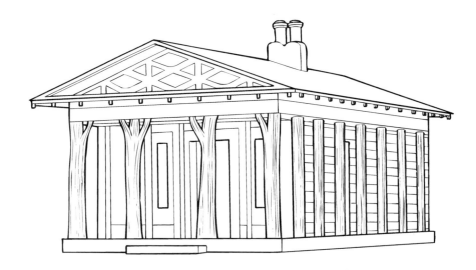

At times, architects freely adapted the Classical forms, introducing uniquely American details. At the height of the Greek Revival period, Alexander Jackson Davis proposed a rustic alternative. His 1837 design for an American cottage depicts a Greek temple with crude tree trunk columns, invoking both the Classical tradition and a quest for the nation's primitive roots.

Later in the century, the traditional details of Corinthian capitals often were changed to reflect American agriculture. When Thomas Jefferson was supervising the design of the United States Capitol in Washington, D.C., he insisted on substituting leaves of American corn and tobacco for the traditional acanthus leaves. The imposing façade of the United States Custom House celebrates New York City's leading role in trade at the turn of the century with forty-four Corinthian columns, each topped by the head of Mercury, the god of travel and commerce.

Left: Cass Gilbert, U.S. Custom House (1899–1907) New York. An imposing Beaux Arts façade with forty-four Corinthian columns, each one topped by the head of Mercury

Above far left: Alexander Jackson Davis, design for an American cottage (1837). Tree trunks are the columns in this rustic American version of a Greek temple.

Architects also experimented with Egyptian columns, which far predate the Greek. Fluted Egyptian columns—a design that originated around 2600 BC—appear in the doorway of the Apthorpe House in New Haven, Connecticut (1837) and in New Haven's Grove Street Cemetery entrance (1848). The Honolulu House in Kalamazoo, Michigan (1860), is a multicultural combination, an Italianate-style home with flattened columns recalling the owner's house in Hawaii.

Right: Andrew Jackson Davis, Apthorpe House (1837), Egyptian Revival columns, New Haven, Connecticut.

Left: Henry Austin, Grove Street Cemetery entrance (1844–48), New Haven, Connecticut. Egyptian Revival columns.

Above: Honolulu House (1860), Marshall, Michigan. An Italianate house with unusual columns reflecting the owner's house in Hawaii.

The Romanesque Revival columns in Henry Hobson Richardson's late-nineteenth-century buildings are also unique. Romanesque architecture first appeared in Europe around the first century AD and, as the name implies, was itself a revival of Roman forms. But the columns are quite different than the Greek orders. Richardson adapted them to his massive buildings, using short, thick columns with richly decorated capitals in elaborate medieval designs. A century later, Postmodernists like Michael Graves created exaggerated versions—thicker, broader, and, at times, even flattened like signboards.

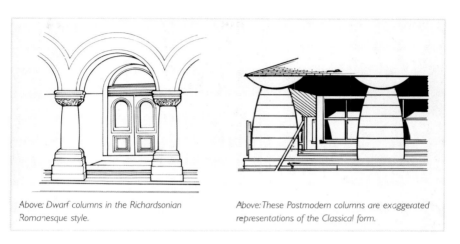

Above: Dwarf columns in the Richardsonian Romanesque style.

Above: These Postmodern columns are exaggerated representations of the Classical form.

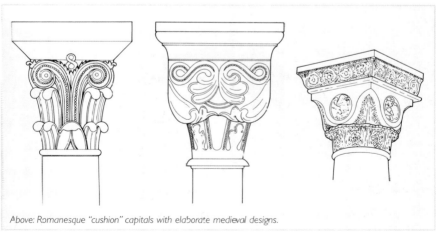

Above: Romanesque "cushion" capitals with elaborate medieval designs.

Twentieth-century architects translated columns into an extensive new vocabulary of design. Frank Lloyd Wright used them to break with Classical tradition and create buildings evocative of Pre-Columbian temples. Unity Temple (1906) in Oak Park, Illinois, is a cubic form that introduced short, sharply cornered columns with abstract designs. The Barnsdale House (1920) in Los Angeles has similar features, which give the house the feel of a Mayan temple. The Art Deco columns leading up to the Merchandise Mart (1931) in Chicago provide a stylish entrance and human scale to this massive building. Columns were rarely seen in the boxy Minimalist homes of the International style, but they reemerged as gigantic features of the modern skyscraper. Many late-twentieth-century towers are elevated on huge columns, creating high-ceilinged street level arcades. One of the first was the Citiccrp Center (1977) in New York, a fifty-nine-story tower supported on four "supercolumns," each ten stories high and twenty-four-feet square.

Right: Frank Lloyd Wright, Unity Temple (1906), Oak Park, Illinois. While most other architects of this period were designing elaborate Classical columns, Wright introduced these cubic forms and abstract designs.

Far right: Frank Lloyd Wright, Barnsdall House (1920), Los Angeles. The columns give the building the feel of a Mayan temple.

Right: Graham, Anderson, Probst, and White, Merchandise Mart entranceway (1931), Chicago. The Art Deco columns provide a human scale for this massive building, the largest commercial structure in the world.

Left: Hugh Stubbins and Associates, Citicorp Center (1977), New York. The fifty-nine-story tower is supported by ten-story-high "supercolumns." The design provides room for a large public plaza under the building.

CHAPTER VII
PORCHES, BALCONIES, AND VERANDAS

A home puts its best face forward with a front porch. Greek porticos, Spanish verandas, and Victorian gingerbread porches are graceful fixtures of American life, providing an impressive entryway or a pleasant perch to overlook family and neighborhood activity.

A porch also sets the tone of religious and civic buildings, offering comfort and shelter or commanding deference and respect.

Right: Gamaliel King, Brooklyn Borough Hall (1848), Brooklyn, New York. Although massive in scale, the Greek Revival portico of this government building is an inviting public place.

While Georgian porticos were often confined to doorways, the porch expanded to its full potential in the Greek Revival style of the early nineteenth century. Greek porticos were the distinguishing feature of this style and more than any other Classical element they changed the face of American architecture. By the Civil War, large Greek porticos spanned the front of southern plantations—and still typify the popular image of those grand mansions. However, small porticos with simple Greek pediments and columns also were used in shotgun houses the long, narrow buildings of African American origin, a little-known yet distinct housing type found in southern states.

Left: Samuel McIntyre, Gardner-Pingree House (1804), Salem, Massachusetts. A beautifully appointed Georgian portico.

*Left: Shotgun house (late nine-
teenth century), New Orleans.
A one-room-wide house with a
simple Classical portico.*

*Far left: Dunleith Plantation
(1847), Natchez, Mississippi.
A Greek Revival portico
surrounds the house.*

Left: Greek Revival house (c.1840), Montague, Massachusetts. Greek Revival pediments and columns were easily added to traditional gable roofed houses.

Far left: Ithiel Town and Alexander Jackson Davis, Russell House (1830), Wesleyan University, Middletown, Connecticut. A monumental full-width portico of Corinthian columns.

Greek Revival porticos were just as common in the North. The Second Bank of the United States in Philadelphia established the Greek portico as a symbol of financial stability. Prominent bankers such as Nicholas Biddle wanted the symbol on their homes as well, and he added one to his Pennsylvania estate, modeled on the Parthenon in Athens. Simpler, yet elegant versions also appeared on more modest homes throughout New England. The region's traditional pitched roof and gable easily accommodated the Classical pediment and colonnade.

For church-going Americans, the beauty of Greek and Roman temples transcended their pagan origins, leading congregations across the country to choose Classical porticos for their houses of worship. One of the earliest and best examples can be found on the church where George Washington worshipped in the early days of the republic, St. Paul's Episcopal Chapel (1764) in New York City. Its magnificent portico was inspired by a London masterpiece, St. Martin-in-the-Fields (1727).

Right: James Gibbs, St. Martin-in-the-Fields (1727), London. A model for American churches in the late eighteenth and early nineteenth centuries.

Far right: St. Paul's Chapel (1764), New York. This church, the city's oldest, was strongly influenced by St. Martin-in-the-Fields in London.

With more historical examples, architects at the start of the nineteenth century had multiple possibilities for Greek porticos—and a whole new vocabulary of architectural terms: prostyle, columns at the entrance; amphiprostyle, columns at each end; or peripteral, columns all around the building. The number of columns ranged from two (distyle) to eight (octastyle) columns across the front of the building.

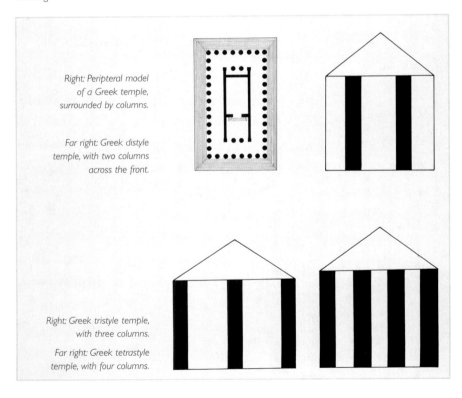

Right: Peripteral model of a Greek temple, surrounded by columns.

Far right: Greek distyle temple, with two columns across the front.

Right: Greek tristyle temple, with three columns.

Far right: Greek tetrastyle temple, with four columns.

Above: Beauregard House (1830), near New Orleans. A country residence with an octastyle (eight column) portico at the front and rear of the house. The balcony reveals the New Orleans influence.

Serenely beautiful and historic, Classical porches, nevertheless, proved to have limitations for domestic use. The tall columns could be formal and forbidding, more suited to a temple than to the everyday activities of family life. Certain areas, such as the Southwest and New Orleans, retained their own traditions. Columned porticos found their way into some early mission churches, such as San Antonio de Valero—better known as the Alamo (1774–56). But the typical western home and church had a Spanish-influenced veranda or balcony. The Larkin House (1835) in Monterey, California, was built at the peak of the Greek Revival period but has a veranda on two stories. New Orleans homes in the same period were built with lacy, wrought-iron balconies, characteristic of the French Quarter. Louisiana plantations often combined Classical and local features, such as Corinthian columns with balcony railings.

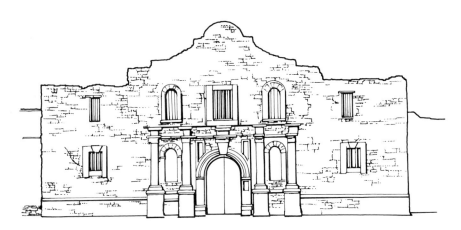

Above: San Antonio de Valero, the Alamo (1744–56), San Antonio, Texas. Classical columns on a Spanish Mission church façade.

Above: Larkin House (1835), Monterey, California. Spanish-style veranda.

Left: Edmond Bozonier, San Francisco Plantation (1856), St. John-the-Baptist Parish, Louisiana. Greek columns on a Spanish-style veranda.

Right: Hillforest, the Thomas Gaff House (1856), Aurora, Indiana. The rounded portico on this Italianate house was custom designed to resemble a steamboat, one of the sources of the owner's fortune.

Classical porticos got their greatest competition from the large, rambling, and wildly individualistic porches that captured the public imagination in the late nineteenth century. Gothic Revival porches introduced gingerbread trim. Later in the century, the High Victorian porches—Italianate, Queen Anne, and Stick styles—were decked out in attention-grabbing details, such as brightly painted, intricately carved brackets and spindled railings. Shingle-style homes often had large, curved porches wrapped in undulating bands of shingles. But Classical porticos became popular once again after the World's Columbian Exposition of 1893. This Great White City of Classical buildings in Chicago reintroduced the style with nationwide fanfare. Well into the next century, stately mansions and civic buildings, such as New York City's main public library, would be built in the Beaux Arts and Neoclassic styles with grand, templelike porticos.

Above: Gothic Revival house, Haddam, Connecticut. The porch has graceful Renaissance Revival arches.

Left: Patterson House (begun in 1850s, enlarged in 1889 and 1913), Fremont, California. A High Victorian porch.

Right: Henry Austin, Villa Vista (1878), Stony Creek, Connecticut. A two-tiered porch in the Stick style. This elaborate porch also has features of the Carpenter Gothic and Swiss Chalet styles.

Below: Henry Hobson Richardson. Paine House (1886), Waltham, Massachusetts. A sweeping Shingle-style porch roof with a rough masonry base.

*Above: Peabody and Stearns,
Stoddard House (1907), New
Haven, Connecticut. A Neoclassical
portico on a stately home.*

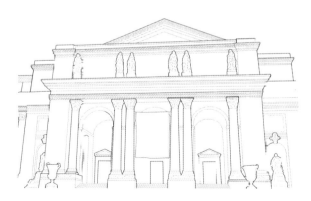

*Left: Carrere and Hastings New
York Public Library (1911) New
York. One of the city's most
famous Neoclassical porticos.*

Modern architects rejected Classical traditions and transformed the portico into projecting canopies, decks, and balconies. The most daring designs employed a construction technique known as a cantilever, the extension of a beam supported at one end only. The unsupported portion carries the deck or balcony. Frank Lloyd Wright used cantilevered balconies as early as 1909 in the Gale House in Oak Park, Illinois. His most famous ones are in Fallingwater (1936), a unique organic-style home in Mill Run, Pennsylvania. Cantilevered balconies rose to new heights in high-rise apartment towers. Some of the earliest and most unusual are in the corn-cob shaped Marina Towers (1964) in Chicago.

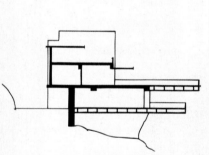

Above: Sectional diagram of Fallingwater, showing the support trusses for the balconies anchored into the hillside.

Left: Frank Lloyd Wright, Fallingwater (1936), Mill Run, Pennsylvania. In this famous example of his organic style, Wright extended balconies over a cascading waterfall.

Above: Bertrand Goldberg, Marina City (1964), Chicago. The semicircular balconies are supported by the cylindrical core of the towers.

CHAPTER VIII
TOWERS, TURRETS, AND STEEPLES

From New England churches to the Brooklyn Bridge and the Chrysler Building, towers express human aspiration. They let us dream of impossible journeys, focus our eyes on the heavens, and even carry us halfway there. Long before the invention of the elevator, towers, turrets, and steeples were our stairways to the stars. Historically, these vertical structures are derived from the Gothic churches and castles of medieval Europe. Religious or romantic, they inspired future generations of architects to reach for the sky.

Although European settlers were steeped in medieval architecture, they built few towers in the first colonial settlements, either for lack of time and materials or out of deliberate design. Spanish colonists incorporated crude towers in seventeenth-century Catholic missions in the Southwest, but the Puritan, Dutch Reformed, and Quaker congregations of New England purposely avoided them as ostentatious show. Their meetinghouses were simple four-square buildings. If a bell tower was used to call members to prayer, it often was a separate structure.

Left: San Xavier del Bac (1783–97), Tucson, Arizona. Elaborate church towers in the Spanish Baroque style.

Far left: John and Washington Roebling, Brooklyn Bridge (1869–83), New York. The bridge towers were the city's first skyscrapers, rising higher and plunging deeper into bedrock than any other structure had done before.

Anglican churches in America followed British models, in particular those by Sir Christopher Wren, who revived the steeple, which had been out of fashion in England since the Renaissance. After the Great Fire of London destroyed nearly a hundred churches in 1666, Wren designed replacements for more than half of them. His basic model is evident in Boston's Old North Church (1723). Its 172-foot-high steeple is the legendary place where two lanterns were lit to signal Paul Revere that British troops were coming in 1775, spurring his famous ride to warn American rebels. Even after the revolution, British churches continued to shape American designs. The most influential model was St. Martin-in-the-Fields by James Gibbs, London's most successful architect of the early eighteenth century. Its soaring tower and steeple were reflected in American churches throughout the next century.

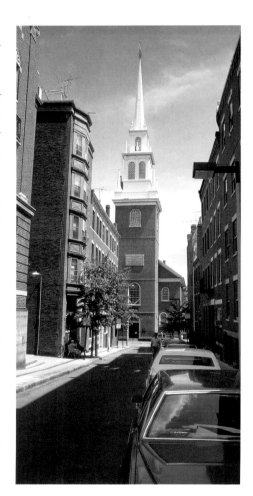

Right: William Price, Old North Church (1723), Boston. This landmark of the American Revolution, the place where lanterns were lit to send Paul Revere on his famous ride, was based on the tower of a London church designed by Sir Christopher Wren.

Left: James Lawrence, St. Paul's Chapel steeple (1796). New York. Now dwarfed by modern skyscrapers, St. Paul's was Manhattan's tallest tower through the first half of the nineteenth century.

Above: Nineteenth-century church steeples combined a variety of forms.

Bottom far right: Henry Fernback, Central Synagogue (1872), New York. Moorish-style tower.

The two major influences on American architecture in the nineteenth century, Greek and Gothic Revival, took off in different directions. While Classical Greek buildings followed the horizontal plane, the Gothic Revival emphasized the vertical, launching an arsenal of towers, turrets, and steeples. Church steeples and towers became increasingly complex with elements drawn from a variety of styles. Steeples were stacked with columns, arches, and balustraces, topped by cupolas with pointed, flared, or domed roofs. Towers at times looked like medieval castles with turreted battlements, or were designed as lighthouses in seacoast villages. Gothic churches had either single or double towers, with central or asymmetrical variations. The Moorish style of domed towers was popular in many synagogues built at the end of the century.

Left: Frank W. Sandford, Shiloh Temple (1897), Durham, Maine. This lighthouselike tower was added to a Second Empire–style church. Built for a small sect called the Kingdom, the tower included a cupola known as the Jerusalem Turret, where members prayed for twenty-four hours at a time

Right: Baptist Church, Ludlow, Vermont. The rounded turrets are characteristic of both the Queen Anne and Shingle styles.

Far right: Andrew Jackson Downing, Llewellyn Park (1853), Orange, New Jersey. The gatehouse has a fairy-tale quality in keeping with the picturesque, romantic characteristics of the Gothic Revival style.

When the Brooklyn Bridge was finally completed in 1883, this great architectural and engineering achievement of the age towered over every building in New York City, soaring upward with Gothic arches. And in the fabulous mansions and High Victorian homes of the city, the motto for towers and turrets seemed to be the more the merrier. Stone towers and turrets abound in the medieval-style castles and chteaux built for mercantile princes and stars of the stage in the late nineteenth century. Wooden varieties, richly decorated and painted, as in the High Victorian Carson House (1886) in Eureka, California, are equally elaborate.

Above: Brooklyn Bridge tower. Gothic Revival arches and rugged masonry were uniquely combined with the airy filigree of steel cables.pearean actor.

Right: Thomas L. Smith, Fonthill, the Edwin Forrest house (1848), Bronx, New York. A medieval castle built for a celebrated Shakespearean actor.

*Left: Richard Morris Hunt,
Biltmore, the Vanderbilt estate
(1889–95), Asheville, North
Carolina. This lavish estate
introduced the Chteauesque
style to America.*

*Left: Samuel and Joseph Newsom,
Carson House (1886), Eureka,
California. This High Victorian
house is an explosion of towers
and turrets.*

Towers disappeared in the low-roofed Prairie houses and boxy International-style buildings of the early twentieth century.

Right: Frank Lloyd Wright, Wingspread, the Herbert Johnson house (1937), tower and cupola, Wind Point, Wisconsin. The stream-lined glass and steel tower functions as a skylight.

Left: Frank Gehry, Norton House (1983), Venice, California. Located on the Venice boardwalk, the house features a fanciful version of a lifeguard tower and provides panoramic views of the ocean.

Above: Daniel Burnham, Flatiron Building (1903), New York. The height of this slender, freestanding tower was a wonderful, yet fearful sight in the early twentieth century. Many New Yorkers, not used to skyscrapers at this time, called it "Burnham's Folly" because they thought it might topple.

But they took on an entirely new shape, scale, and meaning in the skyscraper age. In this new era, the word "tower" became synonymous with an office or apartment building. The Flatiron Building (1903) in New York was not the first skyscraper, but its slablike shape became the first popular image of a modern tower. However, as commercial and religious buildings grew taller, it was sometimes hard to tell one from the other. New York City's Woolworth Building (1910–13) and Chicago's Tribune Tower (1922–25) borrowed the style of Gothic cathedrals, while the Chicago Temple (1924), a Methodist Church with a traditional steeple, was built more than 500 feet in the air on top of a modern skyscraper. The most recognizable spire of the modern age is not on a church, but on the Chrysler Building (1930).

The tower took on a radically different form and function in Chicago's Marina City in 1964. These sixty-four-story twin towers were startling, not only because of their corn-cob shapes, but because they encompassed a new concept of high-rise living. They were cities within a city, a self-sufficient world where one could live, park the car, shop, go to the theater, swim, and even ice skate. The tower was no longer just a building feature, but a lifestyle in itself.

*Left: Holabird and Roche, Chicago
Temple (1924), Chicago.
A church perched on top
of a commercial tower.*

182   ARCHITECTURAL DETAILS

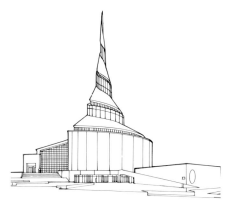

Above: Hellmuth Obata and Kassabaum, Church of Jesus Christ of Latter-day Saints Temple (1994), Independence, Missouri. The modern church is topped by a spiral ziggurat, an ancient symbol of a pilgrim's path.

Right: William Van Alen, Chrysler Building (1930), New York. The silver tower abounds with automobile imagery. The ascending arches on the pointed dome are punctured by triangular windows that suggest the spokes of a wheel. Fabulously modern in its day, the Chrysler Building was the gleaming embodiment of the Jazz Age and the epitome of corporate splendor.

Left: Bertrand Goldberg, Marina City (1964), Chicago The corn-cob shaped towers were some of the earliest mixed-use buildings, combining residential, retail, and office space in the same structures.

CHAPTER IX
MASONRY

Two thousand years ago, Native Americans in the Southwest built their homes with architecture's ancient building blocks—stone and bricks. The stone cliff houses and pueblos of sun-baked adobe bricks still stand, a testament to their durability. Europeans brought another rich heritage of masonry across the Atlantic, but it took time to emerge in the colonies where the most abundant and affordable material was wood.

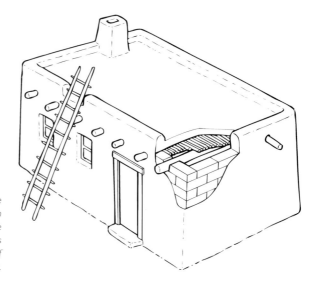

Right: Built from the soil of the Southwest, Native American pueblos like this one date to the first century. The drawing shows the construction method of layering clay over adobe bricks.

With timber always available and stone masons in short supply, the early colonists framed and clad their homes in wood, except for the stone or brick chimneys. Stone houses were common only in Dutch and German colonial communities, where many immigrants were skilled masons. Throughout the colonies, stone was generally the choice of more wealthy homeowners. If masonry was too expensive, builders would create a theatrical illusion by cutting wide wooden boards to imitate stone and mixing sand in the paint to create a rough texture. Thomas Jefferson, the guiding spirit of American architecture, believed that the new republic was sorely lacking in fine masonry buildings. In 1785, he wrote a scathing dismissal of wooden architecture in his native Virginia. "The private buildings are very rarely constructed of stone or brick, much the greater portion being of scantling and boards, plaster with lime. It is impossible to devise things more ugly, uncomfortable, and happily more perishable."

Left: Henry Whitfield House (1639), Guilford, Connecticut. Stone houses like these were rare in the seventeenth century.

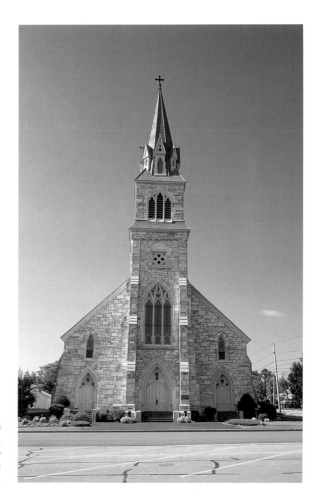

Right: Patrick C. Keely, St. Bridget's
Roman Catholic Church (1861),
Rutland, Vermont. This marble
church features Gothic buttresses
on either side of the tower.

In the early nineteenth century, American architects began to reach for the pinnacle of stone masonry achieved in medieval Gothic churches. Leading them on was a fervent advocate of the Gothic Revival style, Augustus Pugin, whose best-known work is the remarkable detailing on the Houses of Parliament in London. Pugin's persuasive publications found many converts in America. One of the best known is Richard Upjohn, who closely followed Pugin's drawings in designing Trinity Church (1839–46) in New York City. Built of brown sandstone, a locally quarried stone, Trinity Church has a rich variety of Gothic details, including the irregular stones Pugin recommended to create a rich texture. In Vermont, Patrick C. Keely built St. Bridget's with irregular blocks of marble from the state's famous quarries. It also displays prominent marble buttresses, the external supports used in medieval churches.

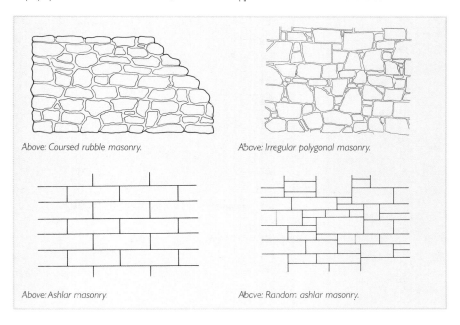

Above: Coursed rubble masonry.

Above: Irregular polygonal masonry.

Above: Ashlar masonry.

Above: Random ashlar masonry.

Right: Andrew Jackson Downing, Gothic Revival chimneys. Elaborately decorated chimneys imitated British designs from the Tudor period.

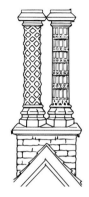

Below: Brown and Von Beren. Stone house (1905), New Haven, Connecticut. This stately Neoclassical home is an example of ashlar masonry.

Later in the century, the British art critic John Ruskin called for a more vibrant Gothic style in rough surface textures and multicolored masonry, known as polychromy. Ruskinian Gothic became one of the dominant styles for public buildings between 1860 and 1880. It is also evident in American High Gothic churches and in the colored brickwork of the Mark Twain House (1874) in Hartford, Connecticut, one of the most elaborate High Victorian houses in America. In the 1880s, Henry Hobson Richardson gave America its own rugged masonry style, using glacial boulders, brownstone, and granite in a striking mixture of shapes, patterns, and colors.

RUSKINIAN GOTHIC STYLE

Left: United Parish (late eighteenth century), Brockline, Massachusetts. The rustic stones and powerful, irregular form of the church are a striking example of the Ruskinian Gothic style.

Right: Covenant Congregational Church (1860), Waltham, Massachusetts. Mid-nineteenth-century English church reform groups exerted a strong influence on architectural styles in America. This model was specifically recommended for a rural church.

Below: Edward Potter, Mark Twain House (1874), Hartford, Connecticut. The colorful, richly patterned brickwork reflects the influence of the Ruskinian Gothic style.

Above: Dwight James Baum, John Ringling House (1924), Sarasota, Florida. Built for the impresario of the Ringling Brothers circus, this luxurious villa has decorative brickwork inspired by the Doge's Palace in Venice.

RICHARDSONIAN ROMANESQUE

Right and above: Henry Hobson Richardson, Brattle Square Church (1869–73), Boston, Massachusetts. Richardson established his rich masonry style in this church. The tower includes sculpture by Frederic Bartholdi, creator of the Statue of Liberty.

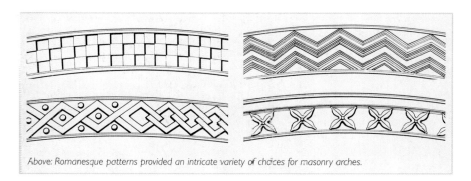

Above: Romanesque patterns provided an intricate variety of choices for masonry arches.

Left: Thomas Annan, Cupples House (1888), St. Louis, Missouri. A lavish mansion built of Colorado sandstone in the Richardsonian Romanesque style.

America finally saw its own magnificent stone cathedrals rise in the late nineteenth century. Two of the best known were built in New York, the home of wealthy patrons and large Catholic congregations. St. Patrick's is a marble edifice largely paid for by the pennies of Irish Catholic workers.

Right: James Renwick, St. Patrick's Cathedral (1858–79), New York. Although the original design was to be built entirely of stone, plaster vaulting was used in some parts of the cathedral to save on costs. Stone buttresses, which might have cracked the plaster, were also eliminated, creating a sleeker appearance.

St. Patrick's elaborate design and huge scale motivated Protestant leaders to begin building their own cathedral, St. John the Divine. Intended to be the largest cathedral in the world, St. John's is still under construction. It began in 1891 in the Romanesque style, but switched to the French High Gothic in 1907. Work stopped during World War II and did not resume until 1980. Local youths were enlisted to learn the art of stonecutting, a program that benefited the neighborhood and also continued the medieval tradition of passing on the craft of masonry to the next generation.

While steel construction eliminated the structural need for masonry, nearly all skyscrapers were still clad in elaborate stone façades, until the advent of the glass curtain wall in the 1950s. The Flatiron Building, the image of a modern tower in 1903, wears an Italian Renaissance dress of limestone, brick, and terra-cotta. The Neo Gothic Chicago Tribune Tower (1922–25) even has flying buttresses. In the 1980s, the Postmodernist Sony Building, covered in 13,000 tons of granite, was a dramatic change from glass towers and sparked a rediscovery of stone façades on high-rise buildings.

Left: Daniel Burnham, façade, Frederick Dinkleberg, Flatiron Building (1903), New York City. The façade designer thought of the tower as a Classical column and divided the decorative cladding into three sections—base, shaft, and capital. This view looks up to the huge capital and its emphatic termination in the overhanging cornice.

Right and far right: Raymond Hood and John Howells, Chicago Tribune Tower (1922–25), Chicago. The Neo Gothic tower is a rare example of a skyscraper with medieval flying buttresses. Connected by arches to the building's crown, they stand more than twenty-four stories above street level.

*Right: Flying buttress from Amiens
Cathedral (1220–1410), France.*

Masonry in the modern age involves not only brick and stonework, but the fluid medium of concrete. Although the Romans had used concrete, it did not play a structural role until French builders perfected the technique of reinforcing it with iron rods in the second half of the nineteenth century. Reinforced concrete would change construction methods throughout the world. Frank Lloyd Wright experimented with concrete in many different projects and was one of the first architects to make it an art form. He used it to build Unity Temple in Chicago in 1904, one of the earliest concrete churches, and to create the spiral form of the Guggenheim Museum in New York City in 1959. He also created precast concrete blocks decorated with textile patterns. These "art stones," as he called them, are the main feature of the Ennis House in Los Angeles (1924) and of other Wright homes and hotels in the West that are some of the most unique houses in American architecture.

Modernist architects sprayed concrete, called gunite, onto steel frames. In later years, reinforced concrete would even replace steel frame construction, particularly in residential buildings where concrete provides a quieter base than the squeaking floors on a steel frame. In 1964, Chicago's Marina City towers became the largest all-concrete structures in the world and are still the largest in the nation.

Above: The spiral shape and unadorned concrete exterior of Frank Lloyd Wright's Guggenheim Museum present a dramatic contrast to New York City's traditional masonry buildings

Right: Frank Lloyd Wright, Ennis House (1923), Los Angeles. The house is covered in precast concrete textile blocks that Wright invented and used as a unique form of masonry. The unusual design has made the house a frequent set for movies, including the 1982 science fiction thriller Blade Runner.

Below right: Frank Lloyd Wright, La Miniatura, the Millard House (1924), Pasadena, California. Surrounded by lush gardens, this concrete block house looks like an ancient temple in Central America.

Below left: Textile patterns used in La Miniatura. The house was built by stacking the concrete blocks together without visible mortar joints.

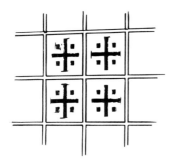

Above: William Rawn Associates, Glavin Family Chapel (1997–2000), Babson College, Wellesley, Massachusetts. The granite block masonry gives this Postmodern building a historic context and provides a highly effective contrast to the glass wall.

CHAPTER X
ORNAMENT

Architectural ornament embodies some of the most creative and original expressions of the artistic spirit. Gargoyles, elaborate ironwork, and intricate gingerbread carvings have no middle ground in architectural fashion—they are either in or out. Through actions and reactions, one style often led to another. Puritans shunned ostentation, Victorians flaunted it. The Arts and Crafts movement rejected the machine, the Art Deco style celebrated it. Modernists stripped away historic details, Postmodernists reinterpreted them. Each age left its own unmistakable signature.

Above: Graham, Anderson, Probst, and White, Wrigley Building (1921–24), Chicago. Four of these huge clocks surround the landmark Wrigley tower. Their enormous tiled faces—two stories high—are an integral part of the tower's great presence on the city's skyline.

Left: John Giaver and Frederick Dinkleberg, 35 East Wacker Drive Building (1926), Chicago. The angel-topped bronze clock on the corner of the building is a perfect ornament for this Neo Baroque building that was built as offices for jewelers.

Ornamental artifacts can speak volumes about the taste and values of their age. A totem pole carved with grotesque animal faces is a key to the complexities of Native American spiritualism. A pendill or wooden pendant was one of the few decorative features of early colonial homes and reflects the value Puritan settlers placed on simplicity. A church pinnacle, encrusted with leaf-shaped ironwork, expresses the organic exuberance of the High Victorian Gothic style.

Left: Northwest coastal plank houses and totem poles, reconstructed Girksan village, Hazelton, British Columbia. Like gargoyles in medieval churches, these totem poles and painted murals are artistic expressions of spiritual beliefs.

Right: Stanley-Whitman House (c. 1720), Farmington, Connecticut. Detail of wooden pendant. These wooden pendants, a tradition in English medieval architecture, were among the few ornamental indulgences in early colonial homes.

Above: These elaborately carved bargeboards, the decorative edging for gable roofs, are a feature of High Victorian houses.

Left: Unitarian Memorial Church (1902), Fairhaven, Massachusetts. Neo Gothic pinnacle encrusted with ornamental iron leaves known as crockets.

"It is the glory of Gothic architecture that it can do anything," John Ruskin maintained in his 1853 book, *The Stones of Venice*. Ruskin's spirit is evident in some of the most extravagant examples of Gothic ornamental detail. The Wedding Cake House (1826/1855) in Kennebunkport, Maine, is an ornate refashioning of a plain Federalist façade into a dazzling display of Gothic woodwork. The owner clearly wanted to break out of his Classical box, and the highly skilled carpenter knew no limits to his artistic reach. He shaped a filigree of gingerbread icing in the style of the Milan Cathedral. The profusely ornamented façade of St. Thomas the Apostle Church (1907) in New York is modeled on the same cathedral and conveys the same unrestrained spirit. The irregular, colorful board and batten siding of Stick-style houses expresses delight in its own version of the Gothic style.

Top left: Thomas H Poole & Co.,
St. Thomas the Apostle Church
(1907), New York. Venetian
Gothic façade in the style of the
Milan Cathedral.

Left: Richard Morris Hunt,
Griswold House (1863),
Newport, Rhode Island. An
extravagant display of board
and batten siding.

Far left: George Bourne, builder,
Wedding Cake House (1826/
1855), Kennebunkport, Maine.
Carpenter Gothic gingerbread in
the style of the Milan Cathedral.

Ornamental features often reveal the common threads that run through the fabric of different styles and periods. The Gothic emphasis on elaborate botanical decoration is also characteristic of two later styles: the Arts and Crafts and Art Nouveau movements of the late nineteenth and early twentieth centuries. These styles are evident in the unique designs of Louis Sullivan. He had a strong belief in the organic origins of art and a deep respect for medieval craftsmanship. Remarkably, he inscribed these age-old traditions in the most modern buildings of his day. His floral, cast-iron ornamentation on the Carson Pirie Scott Building (1899) in Chicago is combined with a broad expanse of modern windows.

Right and far right (detail): Louis Sullivan, Carson Pirie Scott Building (1899), Chicago. The lushly ornamented ironwork is a magnificent foil to the modern expanse of the broad windows.

While the Arts and Crafts movement rejected the machine age, Art Deco buildings ennobled it with sleek lines, geometric shapes, and at times a fantastic sense of humor. The Chrysler Building celebrates the automobile with gigantic hood ornaments and radiator caps that project from all sides of the building like modern gargoyles. A line of hubcaps speeds along the building's striped brickwork. Fashioned of handcrafted steel plates, these ornaments humanized a towering skyscraper and introduced a modern form of craftsmanship. Rockefeller Center, the largest commercial complex of its time, embellished its tailored limestone towers with highly original artwork.

Right: William Van Alen, Chrysler Building gargcyle (1930), New York. A world apart from its Gothic predecessor, this "gargoyle" is a radiator cap for a gigantic car.

Left: Every detail of the Chrysler Building, like this Art Deco glass at the entrance, is expressed with stylized perfection.

WISDOM AND ✳ KNOWLEDGE
✳ ✳ SHALL BE THE ✳
STABILITY OF THY TIMES

Right: Rockefeller Center (1932–40), New York. The buildings in this enormous complex are embellished with artwork focusing on monumental themes.

Left: Stainless steel wall sculpture by Isamu Noguchi on the Associated Press Building in Rockefeller Center.

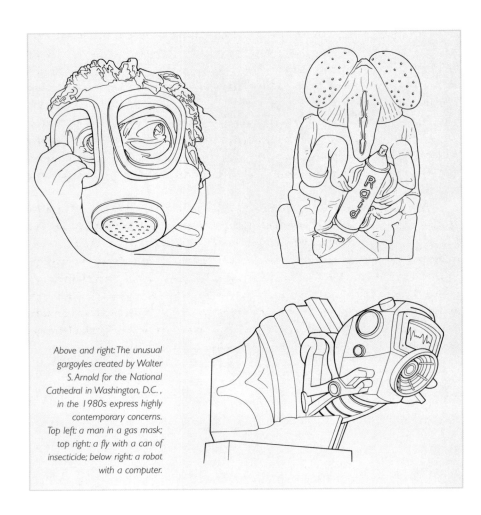

Above and right: The unusual gargoyles created by Walter S. Arnold for the National Cathedral in Washington, D.C., in the 1980s express highly contemporary concerns. Top left: a man in a gas mask; top right: a fly with a can of insecticide; below right: a robot with a computer.

The Chrysler Building was not the first time that gargoyles appeared in a twentieth-century commercial building. The Woolworth Building displayed humorous gargoyles in its lobby in 1913, and the Tribune Tower carried on the medieval tradition in 1925 with an array of gargoyles, grotesques, and animal sculptures on its façade. Some of the Tribune figures are a sly commentary on the journalists and photographers who work in the building, the headquarters of the *Chicago Tribune*. An owl holds a camera in its claw and an elephant, with spectacles, holds its nose, perhaps sensing the smell of scandal. Contemporary gargoyles are also in traditional cathedrals. The ones in the National Cathedral in Washington, D.C., like the grotesque faces on medieval cathedrals and totem poles, express the evil spirits of their own age—a face in a gas mask, a fly holding a can of insecticide, and a robot with a computer.

Postmodern architects have brought back historic ornaments in daring new forms. Although the details are quite different, it is easy to see the connection between Louis Sullivan's cast-iron cornice on the Carson Pirie Scott Building and the elaborate pediment on top of the Harold Washington Library in Chicago. The massive pediment evokes the large scale and intricacy of Sullivan's cornice, and like the master architect's work, the new piece is a bold original. Five gigantic owls, symbols of wisdom, are perched on the pediment. These Postmodern gargoyles are made of handcrafted aluminum sheets welded together and painted green to look like weathered copper. The pediment itself is an extraordinary window, a four-sided glass curtain wall that creates the library's interior winter garden. More than ornamentation, it follows Sullivan's credo, "form follows function."

Left: Harold Washington Library ornament. The thick granite and redbrick walls are embellished with many rich carvings. This one carries Chicago's motto, "Urbs in Horto," City in a Garden.

Far left: Hammond, Beeby, and Babka, Harold Washington Library, (1992) Chicago. Five huge owls, the work of artist Ray Kaskey, are perched on the massive pediment. One sits at each of the four corners, and a twenty-foot-high great horned owl is above the entryway.

The following is an alphabetical listing of some of the most influential figures in American architecture. While a few, such as Vitruvius and Palladio, predate the formation of the United States, each one in this prestigious group has had a major impact on the forms and features of American buildings.

BULFINCH, CHARLES (1763—1844)

America's first architect to work as a professional, Bulfinch was an accomplished designer of Federal-style buildings that shaped the neighborhoods of Boston. He was responsible for many fine Neoclassical buildings, such as the Massachusetts State House (1798), and succeeded Benjamin Latrobe as the architect of the United States Capitol in Washington, D.C. (1817–30).

Right: Charles Bulfinch, third Harrison Gray Otis House (1805–08), Beacon Street, Boston. Bulfinch built three handsome Federalist homes for Otis, the third mayor of Boston and the developer of the city's most fashionable neighborhood on Beacon Hill.

BURNHAM, DANIEL HUDSON (1846–1912)

A leader of the Chicago school of architecture, Burnham was a pioneer in urban planning and exercised great influence over the development of cities across America. With his partner, John Wellborn Root, Burnham designed one of the world's first skyscrapers, the Reliance Building in Chicago (1895). As chief of construction for the prestigious World's Columbian Exposition of 1893, he was largely responsible for making Neoclassicism the dominant architectural style in America through the early twentieth century.

Left: Daniel Burnham, Flatiron Building (1903), New York. Façade detail. The Flatiron Building was the first popular image of a skyscraper, but its ornamental façade reflects Burnham's love of the Classical style.

DAVIS, ALEXANDER JACKSON (1803–1892)

One of the nineteenth century's most prominent architects, Davis began working in the Greek Revival style, but later became the leading proponent of the Picturesque movement, an outgrowth of the Gothic Revival. His masterpiece is Lyndhurst (1838–65), an elaborate Gothic Revival villa in Tarrytown, New York. He collaborated with horticulturist Andrew Jackson Downing (1815–1852) in integrating rural homes into the landscape.

Above: Alexander Jackson Davis, Lyndhurst (1838/1865), Tarrytown, New York. Davis was one of the most important architects of the Gothic Revival style in America. His medieval castle at Lyndhurst has a fairy-tale roofline with pinnacles, turrets, and crenellations.

GROPIUS, WALTER ADOLPH (1883–1969)

Founder of the Bauhaus in Germany, the most influential design and architectural school of the twentieth century, Gropius innovated a revolutionary concept, a new functional interpretation of the applied arts, utilizing glass, metals, and textiles. He came to the United States in 1937 and became professor of architecture at Harvard (1938–52), where he became a spokesperson for the International style in America.

Above: Walter Gropius, Gropius House (1938), Lincoln, Massachusetts. Although Gropius disdained historic styles, his house is now protected as an historic landmark of the International style.

HOOD, RAYMOND MATHEWSON (1881–1934)

Responsible for some of the great signature buildings of Chicago and New York, Hood was the preeminent designer of skyscrapers in the United States during the 1930s. He moved from historicist styles, including the Neo Gothic Tribune Tower in Chicago (1925) and the Art Deco American Radiator Building (1924) in New York City, to sleek modern forms. His major New York City achievements are the Daily News Building (1930), Rockefeller Center (1932–40), and the McGraw-Hill Building (1931).

Right: Raymond Hood with Godley & Foulihoux; Reinhard & Hofmeister; and Harrison & MacMurray, Rockefeller Center (1932–40), New York. Hood worked with a team of architects on this enormous complex of nearly twenty buildings, but he is largely responsible for the sleek form of the centerpiece, the slender seventy-story GE Building, originally called the RCA Building.

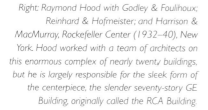

JEFFERSON, THOMAS (1743–1826)

Jefferson was not only the nation's leading statesman—governor of Virginia, minister to France, secretary of state, vice president, and third president—but also the guiding spirit of American architecture. He supervised the design of the United States Capitol, and through his own designs for Monticello, the University of Virginia, and the Virginia Capitol, he sought to establish a new style based on Greek and Roman Classicism as the defining legacy of the new republic.

McKIM, CHARLES FOLLEN (1847–1909)

Together with William Rutherford Mead and Stanford White, McKim founded the architectural firm of McKim, Mead, and White, the leading architectural practice in the United States well into the twentieth century. The firm is known for their great Neoclassical buildings, such as the Boston Public Library (1887–95), buildings at the World's Columbian Exposition of 1893, and New York City's Pennsylvania Station (1904–10, demolished in 1964). McKim also worked on the restoration of the White House and the revival in 1901 of Pierre l'Enfant's 1791 grand plan for Washington, D.C., involving boulevards, formal parks, and monumental public buildings. He was instrumental in founding the American Academy in Rome.

MIES VAN DER ROHE, LUDWIG (1886–1969)

Well known for his dictum "less is more," Mies van der Rohe was a leader of the Modernist style and a pioneer of glass skyscrapers. He established the style in America as professor of architecture at the Illinois Institute of Technology and, in his design for the Lake Shore Drive towers in Chicago (1949), created the first high-rise apartment towers. His later work, the Seagram Building (1958) in New York, is considered to be the premiere example of a perfectly proportioned glass and steel tower.

Right: Ludwig Mies van der Rohe, Seagram Building (1955–58), New York. The shaft of bronze and glass has a powerful and perfectly proportioned form. It led to a sea of glass and steel corporate towers in American cities. The slanted roof of the Citicorp tower (1977) can be seen behind the Seagram Building.

NEUTRA, RICHARD JOSEF (1892–1970)

A leader of the international style and one of the most influential modern architects, Neutra was born in Vienna, Austria, worked for a short time with his architectural hero, Frank Lloyd Wright, in Chicago, and later moved to California in 1926 where he achieved his best-known works. His first Californian commission, the Philip Lovell House (1929) in Los Angeles, is a masterpiece of building technology.

Above: Richard Neutra, Philip Lovell House (1929), Los Angeles Designed for a health and fitness authority, this house of concrete and glass was the physical embodiment of a modern California lifestyle.

PALLADIO, ANDREA (1508–1580)

One of the most important and influential architects of all time, Palladio developed a modern Italian architectural style based on Classical Roman principles that were distinct from the prevalent heavily ornamented Renaissance style. The Palladian style was widely followed all over Europe, most notably by Christopher Wren and Inigo Jones in England. One of Palladio's outstanding works is San Giorgio Maggiore in Venice. His writings also greatly influenced European and American architects of the eighteenth century.

RICHARDSON, HENRY HOBSON (1838–1886)

The first American architect to develop a distinctly personal style, Richardson initiated the Romanesque Revival in the United States. His adaptation of eleventh-century Spanish and French Romanesque became known as Richardsonian Romanesque. He specialized in churches, the most famous of which is Trinity Church, Boston (1877), but also designed other well-known buildings such as the Allegheny County Buildings in Pittsburgh and halls of residence at Harvard.

Right: Henry Hobson Richardson, J. J. Glessner House (1885), Chicago. The rusticated stone walls, rounded arched doorways and deeply recessed windows are hallmarks of the Richardsonian Romanesque style.

SAARINEN, EERO (1910–1961)

Born in Finland, Saarinen emigrated to the United States with his father, Eliel, the leading Finnish architect. After studying sculpture in Paris and architecture at Yale University, he joined his father and Charles Eames in pioneering a new approach to architecture and furniture design. Eero designed many public buildings in both the United States and Europe, including the United States embassies in London and Oslo, the TWA terminal at John F. Kennedy Airport in New York (1956–62), and Washington's Dulles International Airport (1958–63).

SULLIVAN, LOUIS HENRI (1856–1924)

Together with Dankmar Adler, Sullivan established one of the most influential architectural firms in the United States. Leaders of the Chicago school of architecture, Adler and Sullivan built imposing structures with rich detailing and ornamentation, such as the Auditorium Building (1889). They demonstrated an early mastery of skyscraper structure and designed the prototype of the form, the Wainwright Building in St. Louis (1891). Sullivan's other skyscrapers and office blocks in Chicago, particularly the Stock Exchange (1894), Gage Building (1899), and Carson, Pirie, Scott Building (1899), were also far ahead of their time and earned him the title "Father of Modernism." The author of many architectural articles, he is known for coining the adage "Form follows function."

VENTURI, ROBERT (1925–)

A foe of banal modern architecture, Venturi was born in Philadelphia and studied architecture at Princeton University. In the 1950s he worked for Modernist architects Eero Saarinen and Louis Kahn. By the 1960s he was rejecting the blandness of the International style in favor of eclectic and playful designs that incorporated ornament and historical references for their own sake. Venturi helped to establish the tenets of Postmodernism with his 1966 book *Complexity and Contradiction in Architecture*.

VITRUVIUS POLLIO, MARCUS (FIRST CENTURY BC)

Vitruvius was a northern Italian in the service of Emperor Augustus, for whom he worked as an architect, engineer, and writer. He wrote the only surviving Roman treatise on architecture, *De Architectura* (c. 27 BC). A manuscript copy was discovered in the early fifteenth century and it became a standard textbook for Renaissance artists and architects.

WRIGHT, FRANK LLOYD (1867–1959)

Wright is widely acclaimed as the greatest American architect of the twentieth century. Along with Louis Sullivan, he was an early proponent of a distinctly American style, which he introduced in his Prairie-style houses. These long, low buildings merged with the midwestern landscape and their open-plan room layouts shaped the future of modern housing. He continuously experimented with modern materials, including some of the earliest uses of concrete. Although most of his buildings are in the Midwest and California, two of his most innovative are the Guggenheim Museum in New York City and Fallingwater in Pennsylvania. A prolific writer on architectural design theory, he produced writings that were influential on an international scale.

Right: Frank Lloyd Wright, Guggenheim Museum (1956–59), New York. Inside, a cantilevered ramp spirals around the main gallery, rising seventy-five feet to the sky-lit ceiling.

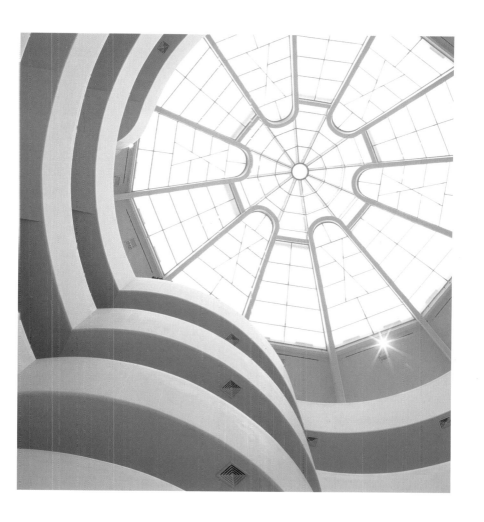

A

abacus On a Classical column, the flat section at the top of the capital, a square block that divides the column from its entablature.

adobe Architecture built of sun-dried bricks found in the Southwest in both Spanish colonial and Native American traditions. The word *adobe* is Spanish and refers both to the mud bricks and, by extension, to the buildings made of them.

A-frame An inexpensive design for vacation homes, with the entire house contained within a steep gable, first designed by Rudolph Schindler in the 1930s.

A-frame

arcade A line of repeated arches supported by columns; they may be freestanding or attached to a building. The term also applies to a commercial gallery of shops, which may be fronted by an arcade or have an interior atrium lined with arches.

architrave The lowest portion of a Classical entablature, this is the horizontal beam or lintel that spans the distance between columns. It is located directly below the frieze.

Arts and Crafts movement A late-nineteenth-century design movement of English origin that sought to counter the trend toward mechanically reproduced ornament and furniture with handmade, artistically designed products. Objects and designs were influenced by the Middle Ages and the art of Japan. This movement had a strong influence on the early work of Frank Lloyd Wright; the Craftsman bungalows of Gustav Stickley and the California bungalows of Greene and Greene are other fine examples.

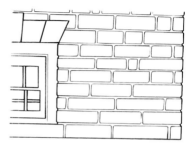

ashlar masonry

ashlar masonry Masonry of regularly cut stones laid in horizontal courses with vertical joints.

B

balloon frame A lightweight framing technique based on the use of standardized lumber and wire-cut nails. Invented in Chicago in the early 1830s, this technique replaced the heavier post-and-beam construction of houses because it was cheaper, faster to

balloon frame

construct, and did not require the same degree of skilled carpentry. The outer walls are sheathed with clapboards or board-and-batten siding. The term was said to reflect the fact that the houses went up as fast as inflatable balloons, or it may have derived from the thin walls.

bargeboard Bargeboards, or vergeboards, are decorative boards, often elaborately carved, on the edge of gables in Gothic Revival houses.

battlement Derived from medieval fortifications, this is a parapet with alternating cut-out and raised portions. Also called crenellation or castellation.

belt course A horizontal course of masonry that marks the division between floors; the raised profile of the course also helps divert rainwater. Also called a string course.

belvedere A separate building or rooftop pavilion for enjoying a landscape view. When separate, such structures are generally called gazebos; those built on rooftops are called belvederes.

board and batten A form of vertical siding comprised of boards laid side by side, with the joints covered with narrow battens for weather proofing. Most commonly found in Gothic Revival architecture.

bracket A projecting support found under eaves, windows, or cornices. Brackets may be used for structural purposes, but they are often merely decorative. They are especially prominent in the Italianate style of the mid-nineteenth century.

bungalow A one-story house with longitudinal plan. The word derives from a Hindustani term for a small house with veranda built for British administrators in India in the nineteenth century.

C

cantilever A beam or truss that is supported at one end only; the free-hanging portion may carry a balcony or part of a building.

capital The top element of a column.

casement window A hinged window that opens outward from the side, rather than having a movable sash; in proportion, it is usually taller than it s wide. These were used in the seventeenth century and revived in the nineteenth century.

cantilever

castellated Describes a parapet decorated with battlements or crenellations.

chinking Clay or mud used to seal up the gaps between the horizontal logs in early houses or frontier dwellings.

clapboard Thin horizontal boards of tapering section used to sea houses against the wind and cold. Such boards covering the clay or plaster surfaces between the half-timbering of the post-and-beam structures of seventeenth-century colonial houses were also called clayboards. The harsh American climate made this additional covering more necessary than in England. Clapboards became one of the most common wall coverings in wood-frame houses.

column A vertical, round, structural post. In Classical architecture, the column usually consists of a base, shaft, and capital.

corbel A projecting stone that carries a weight above it. It may be decorated. A series of progressively projecting stones may form a corbelled arch, or even a corbelled dome, as is found in Navajo hogans.

Corinthian order The most slender and most ornate of the Classical orders; Corinthian columns have an elaborate base and a tall capital that resembles a basket with acanthus leaves growing through it. The height to width ratio of the column is about 10 to 1, and the entablature is about one-fifth the height of the column.

cornice A projecting molding along the top of a building, wall, or arch that caps it off. In Classical architecture, the crowning feature of the entablature.

crenellation See *battlement*.

crocket An ornamental feature of Gothic architecture, this is a small leaf-shaped projection found at regular intervals on the angled sides of spires, pinnacles, and gables.

cupola A miniature domed shape that rises from a roof like a small tower, usually containing windows to let in light or for ventilation.

curtain wall In modern architecture, a curtain wall is suspended from the frame of the building and does not carry any weight, but serves only to shield against weather. The term derives from medieval fortifications.

D

dentil A small square block used in groups (like rows of teeth) for decoration in Classical architecture, typically under a cornice.

dependency A smaller outbuilding that serves as an adjunct to a central building. Also called a flanker in the eighteenth century.

Doric order The oldest and heaviest of the Classical orders. Doric columns have no base, and the capital is composed of a simple abacus and echinus. The height to width ratio of the column is about 4 to 1 or 6 to 1, and the entablature is about the height of the column.

dormer A window set vertically into a sloping roof, with its own separate roof and walls. The name derives from the fact that these were often set in bedrooms.

double-hung window A window with two vertically sliding sashes, or glazed frames, set in grooves and capable of being raised or lowered independently of each other.

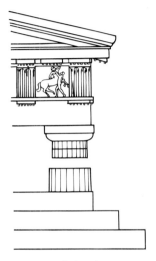

Doric order

dormer

Double-hung windows are of Dutch origin. Frank Lloyd Wright, who preferred casement windows, referred to these as "guillotine windows."

drawing room The term is actually a shortened form of "withdrawing room," where people withdrew after dinner. Found in larger houses of the eighteenth and nineteenth centuries.

drip molding A molded shape designed to keep rainwater from running down wall surfaces; the projecting form breaks the flow of water, so that drips fall away from the wall.

Dymaxion house A round Modernist house designed by R. Buckminster Fuller in 1927, and revised in 1941, to highlight the use of technology and new materials.

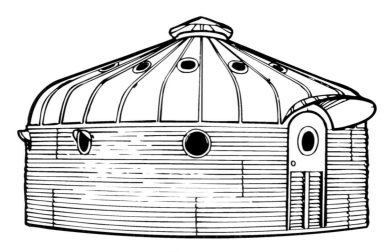

Dymaxion house

E

eaves The projecting end of a roof that overhangs a wall.

echinus The cushionlike molding under the abacus of a capital of the Doric order.

egg and dart An ornamental pattern found in Classical architecture, comprised of alternating ovoid (egg) and arrow (dart) shapes.

egg and dart

elevation A two-dimensional drawing made to show one face (or elevation) of a building.

engaged column A half-column that is set against or into the wall surface.

entablature The upper part of a Classical order, consisting of the architrave, frieze, and cornice.

eyebrow dormer A low dormer of elliptical or segmental arch shape, with a continuous skin of roof shingles covering it, so that it looks as if the roof were raising an eyebrow.

F

fanlight A semicircular or elliptical window over a door, frequently found in eighteenth- and early-nineteenth-century houses.

fascia A flat horizontal band or surface. In Classical architecture, fasciae are found in the architrave.

fenestration From the Latin *fenestra* (window), this generally refers to the use of windows in a wall.

finial An ornamental form found on the top of gables, pinnacles, and canopies in Gothic architecture. The most common shape is a fleur-de-lis.

flanker See *dependency*.

flute The vertical, grooved channel found on Classical columns. The concave grooves are separated by an arris (a sharp edge).

frieze The middle division of a Classical entablature, a horizontal band between the architrave and the cornice. This may be decorated with sculpture.

G

gable The triangular end of a wall below a pitched roof and above the level of the eaves.

gambrel A gable roof with two angles of pitch on each side.

geodesic dome An innovative geometric design for domed houses patented by R. Buckminster Fuller
   n 1954.

gingerbread A term for the ornate scroll-sawn wooden ornaments (e.g. the decorated bargeboards)
   on Gothic Revival houses.

girt A heavy horizontal beam located above the posts in a seventeenth-century timber-frame house.
   Girts are the major beams that surround (circle) the exterior between floors and support the
   floor joists.

guilloche An ornamental pattern of two or more interlacing bands used on moldings in Classical
   architecture.

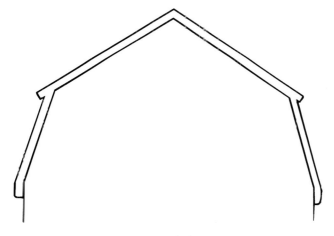

gambrel

H

hacienda A Spanish word for a large estate or ranch; also used to refer to the main house on such an estate.

half-timbering A construction technique by which the house is built with a timber frame (post-and-beam construction), with the spaces between the timbers filled in with plaster or brickwork.

hipped roof A roof that slopes upward from all four sides of the house, rather than ending in a gable.

I

inglenook A recess for a bench or seat beside a fireplace; popular in Shingle-style houses.

Ionic order A more slender and ornate order than the Doric. Ionic columns have a base and a capital composed of scroll volutes emerging from a cushion. The height to width ratio of the column is about 9 to 1, and the entablature is about one-fifth the height of the column.

Ionic order

J

jerkinhead A clipped (or hipped) gable form based on medieval shapes and revived in some American houses of the later nineteenth and early twentieth centuries. It was used for dormers and roofs. The front portion of the gable is clipped and bisected by an angled plane, giving a hooded look to the gable.

jetty (overhang) The projection of an upper story over a lower story, typically found in seventeenth-century New England homes such as the Parson Capen House. These overhangs may be decorated with wooden pendants.

K

keystone The central stone of an arch or vault; see also *voussoir*.

L

lancet A narrow window with a sharp pointed arch found in Gothic Revival architecture.

lantern A small round or polygonal turret crowning a roof or dome, with many windows for ventilation and light.

lean-to A small structure added to the rear or side of a house to provide more space for a kitchen or additional bedrooms. Frequently found in early colonial homes; see also *saltbox*.

lintel The horizontal beam that spans the distance between two columns or posts, or the opening of a window or doorway.

louver In American architecture, one of a series of overlapping boards or narrow panes of glass used to fill a window opening, keeping out rain while allowing ventilation.

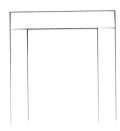

lintel

M

mansard roof A type of roof invented by the seventeenth-century French architect Francois Mansart and adopted in late-nineteenth-century architecture in Europe and America. High and steep, mansard roofs added a distinctive profile and an extra story of space to homes and government buildings.

mansard roof

metope The square space between two triglyphs in the frieze of a Doric order. Usually left blank in houses, it may contain sculpture.

molding A carved or shaped band projecting from a wall or attached to it.

mortise The carved slot in an element of a timber frame, shaped to receive the tenon at the end of another beam or post to make a secure frame.

mortise-and-tenon joint

mullion A vertical element that divides a window into separate lights, or panes of glass.

N

nogging The infilling between the wooden members of a half-timbered house of the seventeenth century; generally of brick, though wattle and daub was also used.

O

octagon A geometric shape composed of eight sides of identical length. Octagon houses were popularized in the mid-nineteenth century by Orson Squire Fowler, a leading advocate of phrenology (the pseudoscience of reading character from the "bumps" on one's head). Thousands of octagon houses were built across the United States.

order Refers to the various types of Classical columns when combined with their respective pedestal bases and entablatures. These include Doric, Ionic, and Corinthian; the combination of elements and proportions within these orders was governed by strict rules.

oriel A bay window on an upper floor, when the bay does not continue to the ground.

P

Palladian window A three-part window construction associated with the sixteenth-century Italian Renaissance architect Andrea Palladio, in which a taller central window with arched top is flanked by smaller rectangular windows. The vertical elements are frequently treated like Classical columns or pilasters.

parapet A low wall placed at the edge of a sudden drop, for instance at the edge of a roof.

pattern book A book containing sample plans, ornamental details, and construction diagrams, popular in the eighteenth and nineteenth centuries.

pediment In Classical architecture, the triangular termination at the ends of buildings or over porticos, corresponding to a gable in medieval architecture, but framed with an enclosing cornice. In later usage, this describes any similar feature found above doors or windows; these may be round, segmental, or broken (open at the top).

pediment

pendill (or pendant) A hanging decorative ornament found on the underside of the overhang, or jetty, of seventeenth-century houses in New England.

piazza In the late eighteenth century, this term was used for a porch.

pier A freestanding solid masonry support, usually thicker than a column.

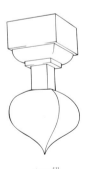

pendill

pilaster A flat column, projecting slightly, attached to a wall. This can be of any Classical order.

pinnacle A small turret or tall ornament that crowns spires, the peaks of gables, or the corners of parapets.

plinth A square or rectangular base for a column or pilaster.

porte cochere A French term for a covered entrance area designed to shield people and coaches from the rain.

portico A porch with a roof supported by columns attached to the main entrance of a house.

prefabrication The use of standardized components, manufactured at a central plant and shipped to the building site for rapid assembly. This allowed the creation of "mail-order" and modular houses in the twentieth century.

Q

quatrefoil Literally, "four leaves"; an ornamental pattern comprised of four circular or pointed lobes. Frequently found in medieval revival styles. See also *trefoil*.

quoins The larger dressed stones found at the

quoins

corners of stone or brick buildings, typically laid in an alternating pattern. Originally used as structural reinforcements, quoins were also used as decorative elements; some American houses used wide cut boards over siding to imitate stone quoins in the eighteenth century.

Quonset Hut An inexpensive prefabricated house with a semicircular vaulted interior; first built at the Quonset, RI, naval base during World War II.

R

rafter A roof timber that slopes upward from the wall plate to the ridge beam.

rafter tails The ends of rafters that project out beyond the walls and are left visible under the eaves of Craftsman-style bungalows.

ribbon window A continuous band of windows, made possible by modern framing techniques, that emphasizes the transparency and open plans of Modernist architecture. A hallmark of the International style.

S

saltbox A characteristic seventeenth-century English colonial house form, comprised of a two-story gabled house with a lean-to

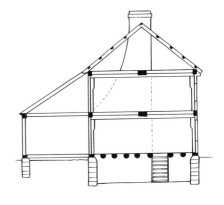

saltbox

addition, which is covered by an extension of the roof that maintains the same steep angle. The term was inspired by the resemblance to seventeenth-century salt boxes. In the South, the roof is also called a catslide roof.

segmental arch

segmental arch A shallow arch based on a segment of a circle smaller than a semicircle.

shotgun house A long, narrow wooden house, usually one story high and one room wide, with a hall running the length of one side. The name is derived from the assertion that one could fire a shotgun through the door and down the hall without harming the interior of the house (it is also called a "gunshot house"). The form may stem from African precedents, after being carried to the West Indies, the Caribbean, and ultimately America, by slaves.

stepped gable Also called a Dutch or Flemish gable this type has a series of steps, like a flight of stairs, along each side of the gable.

stucco An exterior plaster finish made of portland cement, lime, and sand mixed with water and usually given a texture. Frequently used to cover adobe or to give a Mediterranean look over brick, stone, or wood.

shotgun house

swag A carved ornament that imitates a piece of cloth or a garland of fruit and flowers draped between two supports.

T

tenon The projecting tab at the end of a wooden beam or post, cut to fit into the mortise of another element to make a secure joint. See also *mortise*.

tepee A lightweight, portable shelter used by Native American Plains tribes. It is comprised of poles arranged in a conical shape and covered with bark or animal hides.

transom A horizontal bar of stone or wood that separates a door from a window above. Also refers to the crossbar within a window.

treenail An oak peg used instead of a nail to fasten the mortise-and-tenon joints of post-and-beam structures.

trefoil Literally, "three leaves"; an ornamental pattern comprised of three circular or pointed lobes. Frequently found in medieval revival styles. See also *quatrefoil*.

truss A framing element composed of several members joined together to make a rigid structure.

U

Usonian houses A term used by Frank Lloyd Wright to designate his later houses. It is derived from "United States of America" and may also be based on Samuel Butler's Utopian novel, *Erewhon*. Designed to an L-plan, the 1936 Herbert Jacobs First House in Madison, WI, is considered to be the first of the Usonian houses.

V

veranda A roofed porch or balcony, open at the side, with thin supporting columns.

vernacular Also meaning common speech, this is used to denote folk-style architecture, which is based on the common practices of building at the time.

viga A stout horizontal beam used for support in the roofs of adobe structures; the projecting ends are frequently left exposed.

volute The spiral scroll in a capital of the Corinthian order.

voussoir A wedge-shaped block used to form an arch; the central, uppermost one is called the keystone.

W

wattle and daub A structure of woven sticks (wattle) smeared with clay (daub) used to fill in the spaces between the posts and beams of half-timbered houses. This infilling is also called nogging.

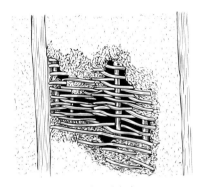

wattle and daub

widow's walk A small observation platform with a decorative railing around it, frequently found on the roofs of eighteenth- and nineteenth-century houses in New England and the Atlantic seaboard. These are popularly associated with seaman's families, but were also used to enjoy the view, even if not near the coast. See also *belvedere*.

wigwam A building type used by Algonquians of the Eastern woodlands area of North America. The wigwam was built on a framework of lashed poles anchored in the ground and bent into an arched or domed shape; the exteriors were covered with bark, reed mats, or thatch. These could be small single-family dwellings or communal structures for several families.

wigwam

BIBLIOGRAPHY & CREDITS

Howe, Jeffery. *The Houses We Live In*. San Diego: Thunder Bay Press, 2002.

Howe, Jeffery. *Houses of Worship*. San Diego: Thunder Bay Press, 2003.

O'Gorman, Thomas J. *Chicago Architecture in Detail*. New York: Sterling Publishing, 2003.

O'Gorman, Thomas J. *New Spaces from Salvage*. New York: Barrons Educational Series, Inc., 2002.

Reiss, Marcia. *New York Architecture in Detail*. New York: Sterling Publishing, 2003.

Editor Marcia Reiss would like to thank the following for their invaluable contribution to *Architectural Details*: Jeffery Howe, Thomas J. O'Gorman, Doreen Enrlich, AbbyMoor and Sandra Forty

Acknowledgments

All illustrations © Chrysalis Image Library / Mark Franklin.

All photographs © Jeffery Howe with the exception of the following images.

T = Top   B = Bottom   L = Left   R = Right

© Chrysalis Image Library 45, 49, 51, 118, 144, 161B, 91, 199 219. / Simon Clay 2BR, 2BL, 8, 9, 60, 68, 69, 71, 77B, 73, 79, 82, 83, 94, 98L, 99T, 100, 117, 120 121 125, 128, 141, 149, 150, 156, 157, 167, 168, 171, 178, 182, 196, 197, 202L, 202R, 210, 211, 212, 213, 216, 222, 224, 229.

© Mark E Gibson / Corbis 107.

© Digital Vision 118, 176T.

© Marilyn Moyer Meditation Chapel, Portland 66, 67. Photographed on the grounds of the National Sanctuary of Our Sorrowful Mother (The Grotto), Portland, Oregon, USA.

© Paul Rocheleau 55.

INDEX